DIPLOMATIC BLOOD FOR TRADE

The Forgotten Price of Opening Japan

SHAWN TENBRINK

ISBN: 979-8-9873592-1-1

Library of Congress Control Number: 2026904421

The views, opinions, and interpretations expressed in this book are solely those of the author and do not represent the official policies, positions, or views of the U.S. Department of State or the United States Government. Any errors or omissions are the responsibility of the author alone.

Cover design by Nada Orlic, erelisdesign.com

Page design by Robert Henry, righthandpublishing.com

Published by Scoutswell

First Edition, 2026

...who once told me that I am the "go-to uncle" for all things old. Thank you for thinking I'm a walking library of cool stories and ancient secrets.

I wrote this for you. One day, when you are old enough to flip through these pages, I hope they spark the same curiosity in you that I feel every day. History isn't just about dates; it's about the people who came before us. I believe that if we don't understand where we've been, it's much harder to see where we're going. May you always look backward with wonder and forward with purpose.

Contents

Author's Note

As a U.S. diplomat who had served in dangerous posts during my twenties, I felt an intense, personal connection to Henry Heusken. He was a young man who, like so many of us who serve abroad, believed fiercely in the mission and promise of American diplomacy. Henry was the first U.S. diplomat ever assassinated while carrying out his official duties. Yet, his name is shockingly erased from our collective memory, his story fading into the obscure margins of history. This book is my desperate attempt to change that.

Henry Heusken's death in Japan in 1861 struck at a pivotal turning point in world history—a moment when the United States was striving to define its place among global powers, and when Japan was only beginning to crack open the doors of its centuries-long isolation. His life and his tragic death embody the fundamental personal risks, profound sacrifices, and towering ambitions that define the American Foreign Service even today.

I have drawn this account from two extraordinary first-hand sources: the candid journal of Henry Heusken himself and the detailed records of Townsend Harris, the first U.S. Consul General to Japan and Heusken's mentor. These journals are invaluable windows into the time—rich in detail, honest in the depiction of cultural discovery, and raw in their expression of human exhaustion. Yet, on their own, they are fragmented. My goal was to weave these fragments together—to forge the facts, the emotions, and the vital historical context into a complete, dynamic portrait of the man and the moment.

In the absence of documented facts, I have not presumed to invent, though occasionally I offer informed conjectures. History, after all, needs no huge embellishment; the truth is already extraordinary. What happened to Henry Heusken—his journey from a Dutch-born interpreter to a central figure in the first American mission, his relentless service beside Harris, and his tragic murder on the dark streets of Edo—is a saga filled with courage, profound cultural conflict, and staggering consequences.

This is not merely the story of a man's death; it is the story of the price paid for opening Japan to the world. It is a story about diplomacy before instant communication, about utter isolation giving way to violent encounters, and about a time when a single man's words could either bridge civilizations or shatter an empire's silence.

Henry Heusken was brilliant, charismatic, and deeply idealistic. He was also human—restless, impatient, and perhaps tragically too trusting. But his ultimate faith was in the power of understanding between nations. For that unwavering belief, he paid the ultimate price. I hope that through these pages, you will come to know Henry as I did while writing this book—not just as a historical figure, but as a fellow diplomat, a bridge between worlds, and a man whose forgotten courage deserves to be fiercely remembered.

I

The Advent of a U.S. Diplomat

"May God protect the *San Jacinto*! May He lead it safely to its destination."

Thus began the first line of the new life, inscribed in elegant French script on October 25, 1855, in the journal of Henry Heusken, a man of twenty-three years whose destiny was now irrevocably bound to the gray, restless horizon of the Atlantic, but would stretch to the Pacific. The heavy steam frigate, a marvel of American naval ambition, was already pulling away from the island city of New York, which he had called home for the past few years.

The pale dawn had just painted the eastern sky the color of a rose, a color Henry knew would soon be exchanged for the blinding, hard saffron of the tropics and, eventually, the alien, impenetrable silence of the Land of the Rising Sun. He stood at the rail, his tall, athletic frame—a Dutch oak among the smaller pines of the crew—absorbing the last sight of the city. The steeple of Trinity Church, silvered by the first rays of the sun, and Jersey and Hoboken, freeing themselves from their veils of night vapors—all signs of that bustling, pragmatic life he was leaving behind—vanished behind the horizon. By boarding this ship of war, he was not merely departing on a professional undertaking; it was an act of faith, a leap into the epic unknown.

For the three preceding years in New York City, he had been trying to live the American Dream, a period of grinding struggle that only amplified the broken promise of his youth. Born Hendrick Conrad Joannes Heusken in Amsterdam, the only son of a soap-maker and merchant, Henry's early life was a lineage disrupted by the brutal, indifferent hand of fortune. At the age of fourteen, while he was away at boarding school in Brabant, Holland, his father, Joannes Franciscus Heusken, died in 1846. The loss was a ruinous event that scattered the family's wealth. As an only child, Henry returned from school at fifteen and attempted to grasp the reins of the failing family business while tending to his sickly mother, but the effort was tragically unsuccessful.

The family business closed, and he found himself working as an office boy in. It was at this time that he decided his future was not in the Old World of Europe and that he would seek his future across the ocean in the United States. This meant leaving his mother, which would be difficult because he was close to her and she was constantly ill and needed constant monetary support from him, but he decided that she alone could not stop him from chasing a better life for himself. Thus, he took a few meager possessions and booked passage on a ship to New York City.

When Henry arrived in America, he found the New World just as hard as the Old. With no family support, no connections, and no money to sustain himself, he took any job he could. He was reduced to small, humiliating jobs that did not even offer enough pay to allow him to afford basic meals. For a man hoping

America would be his fortune, the transition to life in New York City in the 1850s was a cruel shock. The city was a relentless, overcrowded hub where a massive influx of immigrants—predominantly the Irish fleeing the Famine—created a vast pool of cheap, unskilled labor. Finding work often meant grueling, low-paying manual labor like digging roads and sewers, collecting garbage, or working in the burgeoning factories for long hours under deplorable conditions, all while facing the constant threat of unemployment.

Henry would most likely have been immediately trapped in the city's notorious tenements, where entire families and multiple boarders were often crammed into small, poorly ventilated rooms without proper sanitation. These squalid conditions in neighborhoods like the Five Points were rife with noise, filth, disease, and desperation, making mere survival an exhausting, daily struggle. The "American Dream" felt a world away, overshadowed by the reality that his education and refinement were useless currencies until he could make better connections and be given a chance to show himself as something more than a laborer. His greatest assets became his physical endurance and his will to endure the lowliest of roles; the true cost of his freedom was the constant, gnawing hunger and the absolute surrender of his intellectual work in an office in Amsterdam to the brute necessity of earning a few cents a day for a roof and a meager meal.

Fortunately for him, in the 1850s, the descendants of the original New Netherland (the Old Dutch settlers who started New York City), known as the Knickerbockers—a term popularized by Washington Irving that came to symbolize the city's "Old Stock" aristocracy—still had a fondness for Dutch citizens. The Knickerbockers were indeed the quintessential wealthy and connected class, maintaining a formidable grip on New York's social hierarchy, real estate, and banking sectors despite the city's rapid expansion. Families like the Stuyvesants, Van Rensselaers, and Roosevelts occupied the top tier of the "Knickerbocker Trust," priding themselves on ancestral land ownership and a conservative, exclusive social scene that resisted the "new money" of the industrial revolution. Even as their political power began to wane against the rising tide of Tammany Hall, their names remained synonymous with the city's elite institutions and most prestigious addresses.

Over time, Henry started to make connections in the Dutch community, and his gift with the word—even with only an education to the age of fifteen—started to open doors. At this time, he had mastered Dutch, English, French, and German—a quartet of tongues woven into the tapestry of his being, a linguistic arsenal that was his only defense against absolute ruin. This skill, coupled with his manifest qualities—charming, brave, capable, and scholarly—was the very thing that elevated him and gave him an opportunity to move up from ditch-digging. However, it did not suddenly get him great jobs in New York; thus, he was looking for the next opportunity to move up in the world.

As part of moving up, he also decided to not just be a Dutch citizen living in the United States; he wanted to become a U.S. citizen. He was not just stopping by the U.S.; he was here to stay. The decision was not merely practical; it was an act of conviction, a declaration that his fate now belonged to this young, restless republic.

Then, in 1855, Heusken's contacts, most notably the Reverend Dr. De Witt of New York, recognized an opportunity and recommended the multilingual Heusken. It was at this time that Townsend Harris, the newly appointed U.S. Consul General to Japan, the first one the U.S. would ever have there, was in New

York and approached the Dutch community to see if they could recommend a Dutch translator to go with him to Japan.

Within the old Dutch circles, Heusken was quickly recognized as a man of promise, educated, articulate, and driven. His friends saw in him someone destined for more than the modest life of a clerk, someone whose intellect and command of languages could carry him beyond the narrow streets of the city to something greater. With the help of Henry's Dutch community contacts in New York City, they recommended Henry to Harris. Henry had no translator experience and no diplomatic experience, but the community and Harris both must have seen something in him that suggested he would be able to do the job.

Now, it might seem odd that a Dutch translator was needed in Japan, but this is because Japan was a sealed kingdom, isolated from the world for more than two centuries. Their only real contact with the outside world was through their solitary trading partner: the Dutch. During Japan's long period of isolation under the Tokugawa Shogunate's Sakoku ("closed country") policy, the Dutch were the sole Europeans permitted to trade with the islands. From the mid-17th century until 1853, their presence was confined to the man-made island of Dejima in Nagasaki harbor, a tiny outpost that became Japan's only window onto the wider world. Through this narrow channel flowed not just goods, but knowledge—science, medicine, and technology—transmitted through what became known as Rangaku, or "Dutch Learning." While most of Japan remained untouched by foreign influence, a small cadre of officials, interpreters, and scholars devoted themselves to mastering Dutch, translating Western books, and bridging the gulf between East and West.

Neither Henry nor Harris could have anticipated that this recommendation would irrevocably alter the course of their lives. Harris—a man of stern purpose and unyielding conviction who required an antidote of youthful energy—recognized in Henry something far greater than a mere secretary. He saw the essential interpreter, the very hinge upon which the formidable gates of Japan might finally swing open. Though Harris initially believed he was simply hiring a translator to be his sole Western companion in a distant land, the years ahead would forge a bond between them that transcended the simple boundaries of employer and subordinate.

Henry had now been transformed from a normal U.S. citizen trying to live the American Dream in New York City to a U.S. diplomat, the secretary and interpreter to the first U.S. Consul General to Japan.

Harris was a Consul General and not the U.S.'s first Ambassador to Japan because there was a distinction between a Consul General and an Ambassador in the 1850s, rooted in both 19th-century international law and the specific circumstances of Japan's "opening" to the West. At that time, the title of Ambassador was a prestigious rank reserved almost exclusively for exchanges between recognized "Great Powers" like Britain, France, or Russia, who viewed each other as diplomatic equals. Ambassadors served as the personal representatives of one head of state to another, whereas Ministers and Consuls were lower-ranking officials dispatched to nations where full diplomatic parity had not yet been established or where the primary objectives were commercial rather than political.

When Townsend Harris was appointed in 1855, his mission was viewed through this pragmatic lens; unlike Commodore Matthew Perry's earlier expedition which focused on basic supplies, Harris was sent specifically to negotiate the first comprehensive commercial treaty. The United States government designated him a Consul General because his initial role was to secure trade rights and protect American sailors, essentially serving as a functional "foot in the door" rather than a formal political peer to the Japanese leadership.

Although the mission objectives had been clearly defined by the President, the path to securing them remained opaque. However, with the critical acquisition of a second-in-command, the initial uncertainty gave way to action; shortly after his appointment, Henry found himself standing upon the deck of the USS San Jacinto, bound for the East aboard a formidable American warship.

This modern warship, launched in 1850, was an early screw frigate, one of the first U.S. Navy warships to combine both steam power and sail. Visually, she would have looked like a hybrid between an old sailing frigate and an industrial-age steamer. Her wooden hull, tall masts, and square-rigged sails gave her the classic silhouette of a sailing warship, but she also carried a single screw propeller powered by a coal-fired steam engine. The presence of a tall funnel amidships, venting smoke from her boilers, would have contrasted sharply with her otherwise traditional naval lines. She carried around a dozen heavy guns, typically 9-inch Dahlgren smoothbores and smaller pivot guns, arranged along her gun deck and on pivots for broader firing arcs.

The *San Jacinto*'s crew usually numbered between 250 and 300 men, including officers, seamen, engineers, and Marines. The crew was divided into watches to ensure the vessel could operate continuously, day and night. Sailors managed rigging, sails, and gunnery, while the new class of engineers and firemen tended to the boilers and engines below decks—hot, dirty, and dangerous work. Officers had small private cabins, but most enlisted sailors slept in hammocks slung between beams in the gun deck, which doubled as both sleeping quarters and battle stations. Marines served as both security and soldiers, maintaining discipline and providing a fighting force during boarding or landing actions.

Life aboard was crowded, noisy, and uncomfortable, especially on long deployments. Coal dust and smoke from the engines coated everything, and ventilation below decks was poor. Food was preserved and monotonous, salted meat, hardtack, beans, and fresh water was limited. Disease, heat, and the ship's constant motion made life difficult. Still, sailors took pride in serving aboard such a modern vessel; the *San Jacinto* represented the cutting edge of naval technology at the time, bridging the gap between the Age of Sail and the steam-powered ironclads that would soon dominate the seas.

Henry, a man whose prior life had been that of a normal citizen, now found himself utterly out of his element, yet officially integrated among the ship's officers. He had never before set foot on a naval vessel, let alone a U.S. warship bristling with cannon and crew. His initial anxiety was compounded by the fact that Townsend, his boss, guide, and principal companion on the diplomatic mission, would not accompany him for the first leg of the journey. This meant Henry, a relative novice to both diplomatic affairs and the sea, was left to navigate the rigid hierarchies and strange customs of military life alone.

In lieu of the transatlantic crossing, Townsend opted for the swifter yet more grueling passage eastward, journeying through England and across the Mediterranean before traversing the hot overland route through Egypt. He wanted to make stops along the way and meet with officials on his way to the Far East. The plan was for the two to reunite before the expedition's official first stop in Siam (modern-day Thailand), a critical kingdom in the region and the start of their grand diplomatic mission. For Henry, this initial transatlantic crossing was his baptism by fire aboard a ship of war—not merely as a passive passenger, but as a formal participant in a great, official enterprise that carried the flag and authority of a powerful new nation.

As the vessel pulled away from the American shore, the Atlantic waves—the very same he had crossed in poverty and despair a few years prior—rose to meet him once more. A sudden, solemn clarity descended upon Henry, bringing a profound sense of perspective. He reflected on the ephemeral nature of all things human: the vigor of youth fades into age, the allure of beauty to dust, and the sharp edge of brilliance to frailty. His own journey, from educated European to impoverished immigrant and now, improbably, to diplomatic envoy, exemplified this human transience. Yet, beneath him, the Ocean—ancient, timeless, and untamed—rolled on with the same indifferent majesty it had since the dawn of time. Aboard that eternal, humbling sea, he now sailed, his personal destiny interwoven with a mission as vast and enduring as the waters themselves: to forge new relationships between the West and the ancient kingdoms of the East, a diplomatic charge that felt monumental against the backdrop of the immutable deep.

The Passage of Desolation and Hope

The passage from New York to the Far East was not direct. The ship would need to make stops on its way east to resupply with food, water, and coal to drive the ship and feed the crew across the high seas.

The first weeks were a dance with the ocean's temperament. One morning, near the end of October, the frigate encountered a desolate vision: an abandoned ship, moving towards them with its planking ripped away, a skeleton devoid of human sound, save the wind whistling through its rigging. It was salty tears—the tears of the orphans and wives seeking hope from a lost vessel. It was a grim metaphor for the old, rotting, isolationist world they were sailing toward, a world that soon had to be either saved or mourned.

Henry, ever the keen, philosophical observer, found amusement in the contrast between his romantic intensity and the dull practicality of his companions. He mocked the young officer who filled his diary with a mere mathematical inventory of the ship, believing the journal of a life should be a chronicle of feeling, not figures, comparing it to the relentless, unpoetic pursuit of balancing debit and credit in the smoke-filled, polluted atmosphere of a city. He preferred the pure, free air of the ocean to the forced gaiety of New York cafés.

The first respite on the voyage east came on November 11, with the sighting of Madeira. In the 1850s, the island of Madeira was a remote yet flourishing outpost of the aging Portuguese Empire, famed for its stunning scenery, mild climate, and especially its wine. Located in the Atlantic Ocean about 600 miles southwest of Portugal, Madeira served as an essential waystation for ships traveling between Europe, Africa, and the Americas. Steamers and sailing vessels alike often stopped there to take on provisions, fresh water, and—most famously—barrels of Madeira wine, which was prized around the world for its rich, fortified flavor that improved with long sea voyages.

The island itself presented a striking sight to any approaching mariner. Steep, emerald-green mountains rose almost directly from the sea, their slopes terraced with vineyards and banana groves, dotted by whitewashed houses with red-tiled roofs. The capital, Funchal, nestled along a natural harbor on the island's southern coast, was a picturesque town with cobbled streets, small churches, and bustling markets. British merchants and expatriates formed a notable community there, influencing local culture and trade. Elegant villas surrounded by gardens filled with exotic flowers gave the town an air of genteel prosperity.

For Henry, after seventeen days confined to the ship, the sensation of standing on terra firma again was delicious—a joyous relief for a man who did not boast at all that the sea was his element. He found the island was a land of contradictions: the sweet fragrance of flowers and the captivating beauty of its mountainous slopes were guarded by a besieging crowd of child beggars asking for handouts from anyone who disembarked from their boat.

Henry's brief leave on shore was a burst of youthful energy, charging through parts of the island on a galloping steed, clinging vigorously to the pommel, seeing only beauty in the lush quintas, banana trees, and orange groves. Yet, he saw the dark reality too: the oil lanterns barely illuminating the winding, narrow streets, the tantalizing glimpses of Portuguese women behind careful blinds, and the tragedy of the vineyards, where a destructive disease consumed the grapes and left only maggots and no sweet wine—a grim reminder of life's fragility and the sudden, merciless ruin of prosperity.

The Shadows of Empire

Henry's ship only stayed for a short time, and thus the voyage continued, but it did not stop everywhere Henry wanted. He raged at the Commodore's decision to forgo St. Helena, denying him the chance to devote an hour to the tomb of Napoleon, the great General whose legacy fueled Henry's own heroic, world-changing aspirations. Instead, they faced the arid desolation of Ascension Island, a barren rock covered in lava and broken beer bottles, where the only signs of life were the terns—the sea swallows—who nested in the Wideawake Fair. Here, Henry saw the dark heart of man, as sailors from the ship would amuse themselves by throwing stones at trusting little winged creations. Henry noted that civilized man was often a greater beast than the instinct-driven wolf.

Departing Ascension Island on December 12, 1855, Henry headed towards the Cape of Good Hope. He would spend his first Christmas and New Year entirely at sea. Christmas Eve passed quietly, if warmly—a tropical warmth that brought no snow or the cheerful clatter of sleds on New York streets. The prospect of a festive feast was a poor consolation: a somewhat spoiled ham, a few old potatoes, and the shadow of a plum pudding were to mark the day. Yet the heat, stifling as it was, brought a strange comfort, and Henry lay down that day, letting his thoughts drift to distant places and bygone times.

In his dream, the fire burned brightly in a familiar room. Faces from childhood smiled at him, the laughter of family echoing through the years. He imagined a little boy, caught in the joy of Christmas, innocent of the separations and losses that time would bring. How cruelly mistaken youth is, he thought, to believe these moments eternal, unaware of the empty chairs that the future will place among loved ones.

However, this dream was shattered by a drum banging reverie, rousing the crew to battle stations for a simulated night attack. After the drill, he was back in bed among strangers; the child from his memory had grown into a man burdened by recollection, isolated except for the vivid, living pictures of his past. Grim reality pressed close, yet in sleep, Henry could still seek the warmth and happiness of the Christmases that had shaped him.

On January 12, 1856, after thirty-one days at sea, the Cape of Good Hope appeared. For the young American, this was more than a port of call; it was a journey into the ghosts of his ancestry as a Dutchman. In the 1850s, Cape Town was a bustling colonial port at the southern tip of Africa, marked by a distinctive blend of Dutch and British influences. Originally founded by the Dutch East India Company in the 17th century, it had been under British control since 1806, and by mid-century the city reflected both heritages: Dutch-style gabled houses stood beside British government buildings and churches, while English law and administration governed a population that still spoke a rough Cape Dutch dialect—an early form of Afrikaans—in homes and markets.

The harbor teemed with sailing ships and the new steamers stopping to refuel on their way between Europe, India, and the Far East, making the town a crossroads of cultures, sailors, and merchants. British settlers, soldiers, and officials mingled uneasily with long-established Dutch-descended farmers (Boers) and the diverse local population of freed slaves, indigenous Africans, and mixed-race Cape Coloured communities. The result was a city both vibrant and divided—cosmopolitan yet colonial, where

English ambition and Dutch rootedness shaped the character of life beneath the looming slopes of Table Mountain.

The sound of the Dutch language, even in a coarse dialect, struck Henry's ears with pleasing familiarity. He saw the dismal remains of the old fortress of Muizenberg, its cannons half-buried in the sand, and felt a profound melancholy for the fallen greatness of Holland. He wondered: if guns could blush, wouldn't they find an echo in poor Holland herself, this shadow of the past?

Yet, amidst this decay, he found warmth. He enjoyed the true hospitality of the Dutch families in the city and visited them in their homes, noting the high ceilings and spacious rooms of the old architecture. He met and walked with Miss Cloete, a lovely young Boer lady, through the groves of myrtle—a symbol of love—on the high plateau of Constantia, savoring the peaceful rapture that only the society of women could provide. He mused that only women knew how to scatter roses on the path of man, dominating his evil inclinations and cultivating his mind. Here, among his kinsmen, he felt a pull, a desire to reside and get acquainted with his charming feminine "cousins." However, he could not stay.

Before leaving the Cape, he penned a philosophical plea for humanity:

Why did hospitality, this lovely virtue, disappear from the Earth, and why can it only be found in the most remote regions? Oh, Civilization! When will you cease making barbarians of us?

He reflected on the very nature of welcome. In the great, hurried cities of the West, "hospitality" was often merely commerce disguised as courtesy—a trade of favors, a calculated investment in influence. He had found shelter in New York only through the Dutch community's transactional system: work for money. Yet here, at the Cape, among kinsmen who called him Oom (uncle) or Neef (cousin), the welcome was unconditional—a demonstration of that rare, ancient virtue that places the welfare of the guest above personal gain. Pondering the vastness of the world, Henry realized that true, generous hospitality seemed to survive only in those remote regions, far from the competitive, corrosive heart of empire. It was a virtue of the simple, the self-assured, and the enduring.

His time at the Cape came to an end, and he headed to his final stop before the East at Île de France (Mauritius). The sight of the island's shore struck him with a profound literary resonance. Immediately, he recognized the landscape of Bernardin de Saint-Pierre's immortal tragedy, Paul and Virginia—the sharp peaks, the Pouce, the Pieter Both. It was here that the story of pure, doomed love unfolded, a tale of innocence lost that had captivated European romantics. The island was more French than ever, a true consolation for the European soul, where one could revel in the sounds of "Garçon!" and debate the merits of theater and beautiful France. Henry, whose own heart was perpetually seeking the grand, poetic narrative, felt the air charged with the ghosts of the lovers. It was a place where human passion, even in defeat, achieved immortality, and Henry pondered the kind of epic love that could transcend the boundaries of life, death, and even isolation.

The Last Shore of the West

The journey ended in the heat and lushness of Point de Galle, Ceylon (March 6, 1856). The immense, still-solid walls of the old fortress stood as a memorial to three centuries of conquest—Portuguese, then the Lion of Holland, now the unicorn of Britain. There he met a Dutch innkeeper, Monsieur André, a man whose features were familiar yet whose eyes held the weary sadness of exile. André, whose family had deep roots in the colony, poured Henry a genuine gin and bitters, sighing over the Dutch flag that no longer flew over the battlements of Point de Galle.

"Ah! The Dutch," André whispered, leaning in conspiratorially. "We knew how to govern with an iron hand and how to keep the natives within the limits of respect and obedience! Even today, the Hindus address the descendants of the Dutch families with the deepest respect!"

But then his face clouded, the pride giving way to a grudging honesty. "But which of the three nations was the best liked? Well, that is certainly the British. They were the ones who abolished slavery, and they gave equitable laws." He raised his glass in a salute to the pragmatic success of his rivals. It was a painful distinction: the Dutch were remembered for the strength of their domination; the British, for the justice of their administration. Henry understood: the nostalgia for the tricolor was deep, but the welfare of the colonized people—however grudgingly recognized—was better served by the methodical, unromantic rule of English law.

Most crucially, he visited the home of Don Nicholas Dias, a Sinhalese gentleman—a man of quiet dignity who possessed a keen, intellectual curiosity. The native host showed Henry the beautiful ornaments and patiently detailed the ancient customs of Ceylon. He also delivered a sharp lesson to Henry. He spoke not of conquest, but of conscience, observing colonial behavior with weary clarity: "We do not see that you Christian people live better than we do," Dias stated, his voice devoid of anger, merely observation. "Before judging a faith, we judge of its works."

This statement struck Henry with the force of irrefutable truth. It was the distillation of every moral compromise he had witnessed, from the welcome of the Dutch in South Africa to the cruelty on Ascension Island. Dias held up a mirror to the West: the magnificent clockwork of its civilization—its science, its commerce, its theology—was rendered meaningless by the visible greed and violence of its messengers. Henry, the advocate of progress, knew that in the sealed Kingdom of Japan, this maxim would be their ultimate judge. The Shogun would not be impressed by the Bible's words, but only by the foreigner's moral fiber.

Henry saw the wisdom in this. The man who had struggled in New York, who had mourned the lost genius of Napoleon, now understood that his mission was not merely about opening a port or forcing a treaty, but about meeting a mysterious civilization with the respect that his own countrymen rarely showed. The chosen one was not chosen for force, but for his ability to understand.

With the dark, copper-skinned Hindus and the Muslims of the Bazaar behind him, and the phosphorescent glow of fireflies lighting his final walk through the palm groves, he knew for sure he was no longer in the West and would need to adapt.

On March 11, 1856, as the fertile island disappeared from view, he stood upon the deck of the *San Jacinto*, now bound through the slumbering waves of the Indian Ocean for Siam, the next step on his way to the Land of the Rising Sun. His romantic wandering life was over. The great quest had begun.

2

The Meeting of the Mentor

The long sea voyage, undertaken without his companion, had been a significant trial for Henry, but the arrival at Penang was nothing less than a rebirth. Henry Heusken, the young adventurer whose destiny now weighed on him like a suit of armor, stepped ashore on March 21, 1856, into an atmosphere entirely unlike the West he had left. Penang, a colonial jewel of the East Indies, served as his initiation into the heart of the Orient—a world of fragrant spices, debilitating tropical heat, and profound, ancient contradictions. He aptly called it the "Pearl of the Indies," a small, pygmy island where the wealthy nabobs of Calcutta came to seek refuge in the cool, aromatic air of its mountains, yet one whose fate had been callously traded away to the British as a mere dowry of empire.

The American Consul, a man named Currier, proved to be the quintessential host, his table groaning under the bounty of the Indies and the luxuries Europe sent to be plundered. But the true balm for Henry's sea-weary soul was not the food, but the pilgrimage he made daily, five miles by palanquin, to the foot of the mountain. There, a brook, fed by a cascade that leaped and foamed from granite stone, poured into a pool nestled in a grove of nutmeg trees.

What a pleasure, when hot and tired, to immerse oneself, even in the "encumbrances of civilization"—his clothes—into that fierce, purifying torrent! The water, clear and purer than any filtered by the grandest governments of the world, poured over him. He had to huddle against the rock, lest the current, strong as a man's will, carry him away into the swift rapids. He emerged another man: electrified, every pore breathing, before cutting a hole in a freshly picked coconut and drinking its milk in a single draught. This was living, he had scribbled in his journal. This was the life of the savage, and the savage, Henry surmised, was not as deprived of common sense as he might seem.

It was in this atmosphere, ripe with renewed strength and intellectual vigor, that Henry Heusken finally encountered the man who was both his master and his fate: Townsend Harris, Plenipotentiary of the United States to the Court of Siam and Consul-General of Japan.

The Quiet Authority

The meeting took place within the civilized sanctuary of Consul Currier's house, far above the sweaty chaos of the port below. Harris was waiting.

Henry, still young enough to be struck by the physical presence of a great man, beheld a figure of distinguished and dignified reserve. Harris possessed a tall, lean build and a disciplined temperament, and his reserved posture and formal attire immediately made that evident. Though his face was now framed by a full, venerable white beard and white hair, Henry felt the impact of a quiet strength—a composure that hinted at great, contained power. He did not possess the casual arrogance of a born aristocrat, but the weary, purposeful dignity of a man who had forged himself through sheer will.

He was an American product, a distillation of enterprise and self-made grit. He had been born in the modest village of Sandy Hill, New York, in 1804. His formal schooling had been limited to a local primary house, yet his mother, Eleanor, had cultivated in him a lifelong, voracious love for reading and learning. Harris was an autodidact—a self-taught scholar—who had left home at thirteen to join his brother's porcelain import business in New York City.

By sixteen, he was a junior partner, immersed in the meticulous work of record-keeping, but in the evenings, by the dim light of his lamp, he was traversing worlds far grander than his ledger books. He taught himself French, Spanish, and Italian. His mind was a restless engine of curiosity, extending from literature to natural history.

But Harris' ambition, Henry realized, was not to amass wealth, but to open gates. He had used his commercial success to serve the public good, becoming the respected President of the New York City Board of Education in the 1840s. It was Harris who championed free education for all, arguing passionately in the newspapers under the proud pen name, "Plain Truth," and who played the leading role in founding the Free Academy of the City of New York (later City College)—a tuition-free beacon for the children of the city's working class.

He was a man who believed in the betterment of the world, not through abstract philosophy, but through the difficult, tangible work of trade and education.

The Necessary Man

In 1847, as if the confines of New York City had become too small for his expansive mind, Harris abandoned his business, bought a ship, and plunged into the raw, exhilarating chaos of Asian trade, sailing the ports of China and the Dutch East Indies. He was already a diplomat of commerce before he became a diplomat of state—a man who understood the rhythm of the East, the subtle interplay of profit and custom.

This long, patient apprenticeship was precisely why President Franklin Pierce had appointed him on August 4, 1855, as the first U.S. Consul General to Japan. He was the man for the pivot: experienced, trustworthy, and possessing the diplomatic potential to capitalize on the half-opened door left a few years earlier by Commodore Perry.

By late March and early April of 1856, however, the date of his appointment felt a world away. Harris and Henry now found themselves in Penang, where they spent their days immersed in strategy, maps, and the dry details of diplomatic protocol within the cool confines of the Consulate. This period of intense preparation was punctuated for Henry by invigorating dips in a mountain cascade, but eventually, their time in Penang drew to a close.

On April 2, 1856, Henry and Townsend departed Penang, the small island gradually shrinking into the distance as the USS *San Jacinto* cut through the waters of the Straits of Malacca, skirting the southernmost tip of Asia. Two days later, they arrived at Singapore, a port that had sprung from near nothing in the span of forty years—a living testament to the power of free trade, the very principle Harris and Henry were determined to bring to Japan.

Singapore's harbor was a sprawling spectacle of global commerce, where Chinese junks with taut, ribbed sails drifted alongside vessels flying the red ensign of His Magnificent Majesty of Siam, the iconic white elephant emblazoned at its center. Amidst this forest of masts, British, Dutch, and French ships jostled for space, their presence a stark reminder of Europe's tightening grip on the Indies.

Dominating the inner harbor lay a French squadron—a pair of traditional corvettes and a modern steam corvette—acting as the silent, iron-fisted sentinels of empire. These sleek, three-masted warships represented a navy in transition: while they still carried eighteen to twenty-four guns on a single flush deck like their sailing predecessors, the newer steam corvette boasted an innovative retractable screw propeller and a coal-fired engine. Resting low in the water between the heavy frigates and light sloops, these vessels signaled to every traveler that in this bustling corner of the world, diplomacy was always backed by the looming threat of modern force.

On shore, the city revealed its own contrasts. The London Hotel, though not famed for culinary excellence, offered modest prices that were a welcome consolation for weary travelers. Along the esplanade, a broad seafront promenade, the tropical sun glinted off the waters while merchants and laborers moved with tireless energy. Henry and Harris explored the famed Chinese Pagoda and visited the house of the illustrious Whampoa, a merchant whose influence spanned the region. His residence, blending European architectural styles with Chinese sensibilities, spoke to the city's cosmopolitan character. Only four decades prior, Singapore had scarcely existed; now it thrummed with life, a magnet for commerce precisely because it embraced openness and free trade—an openness the Dutch had stubbornly resisted with their restrictive and ultimately self-limiting policies.

Singapore was, to Henry and Townsend, more than a port—it was a living lesson in the potential of commerce and diplomacy, a vivid demonstration of what could be accomplished when barriers were removed and the world allowed to meet itself on common terms—a testament to the power of free trade that Harris and Henry were determined to bring to Japan.

3

The Apprenticeship in Siam

The seven-day sail from Singapore to the roadstead of Siam was the final calm before the diplomatic storm. When Henry and Townsend arrived in Siam (modern-day Thailand), it was an independent kingdom in Southeast Asia, ruled from Bangkok by the Chakri dynasty, with King Mongkut (Rama IV) ascending the throne in 1851. The government was an absolute monarchy, though it relied on a complex bureaucracy of nobles and mandarins who administered provinces, collected taxes, and maintained law and order. While the king wielded ultimate authority, local governors exercised considerable autonomy, particularly in distant regions, reflecting a balance between central control and traditional provincial power. Diplomacy was a critical concern: Siam carefully managed its relations with European powers and neighboring kingdoms to maintain sovereignty amid growing colonial ambitions in the region.

Economically, Siam was largely agrarian, with rice cultivation forming the backbone of wealth and sustenance, supplemented by fishing, teak and forest products, and small-scale handicrafts. Trade was expanding, however, particularly in

Bangkok and the Chao Phraya River port, where foreign merchants—including the British, French, Americans, and Chinese—conducted business in rice, teak, and other tropical commodities. Culturally, Siam was deeply Buddhist, with temples (wats) at the heart of communities, influencing daily life, education, and governance. Traditional arts, architecture, and music flourished alongside cautious adoption of Western technology and science.

Under King Mongkut's progressive vision, the country began cautiously modernizing infrastructure, surveying the land, and opening itself to foreign knowledge, laying the groundwork for the diplomatic and commercial engagements that figures like Townsend Harris and Henry Heusken would encounter, but the approach to the capital was itself a plunge into the deep, fragrant heart of Asia.

On April 14, 1856, after the *San Jacinto* had anchored off the mouth of the Menam River—the Mother of Waters—a small, smoke-belching steamboat, the *Royal Seat Siamese Steam Force*, came to fetch them. They were enveloped in the roar and sulfurous cloud of a seventeen-gun salute fired in honor of the Ambassador, a final, Western expression of power before they submitted to the customs of the Siamese Court.

Harris, severe and composed in the tropical heat, viewed Siam as a necessary staging ground. He was here as plenipotentiary for two reasons: to successfully conclude a treaty (a diplomatic footnote to the massive task ahead) and, more importantly, to give Henry Heusken his baptism by fire in the art of the Treaty.

Harris had no time for failure. The Siam mission was smoother than Japan would be, due to the precedent set by European diplomats like the British, who already had treaties with Siam. For Henry, this was his apprenticeship—a controlled environment where he could observe, absorb, and learn the subtle language of negotiation, a skill far more critical than his native Dutch.

The sixty-mile journey up the Menam was hypnotic. The river, wide and lazy, was the highway of the kingdom, its banks thick with jungle, palm trees, and the graceful, slender arecas palms swaying above bamboo huts built precariously on stilts. Henry watched, fascinated, as the King's enormous Cochin Chinese boats, powered by one hundred and forty oarsmen, cut through the water, accompanied by a band whose music was as foreign as the air itself.

Upon reaching Bangkok, Henry noted with an immediate, critical eye the Siamese government's efforts to impress. They were quartered in a large, new bamboo house with seven bed-rooms—the first hint of the King's modernization effort. The food, however, was a trial. Chickens, ducks, and curries were smothered in garlic to an extent that would make a Provençal weep, a culinary assault Henry deemed a fault not of the Sia-mese, but of the immense gulf separating their way of life from civilized nations.

Yet, there were wonders: the fragrant, beautiful fruits sent continually by the two Kings and the nobles. Henry cherished the mangosteen, comparing the melting, snow-white balls with-in their pink shells to the lips of young Malayan girls—the most exquisite, delightful fruit of the tropics. Its detestable counter-part, the durian, was, to Henry's nostrils, the *essence of all the refuse of the world*, forcing him to hold his nose. However, he recognized the sheer power of human habit that eventually allowed Westerners to convince themselves it was delicious.

The Theatre of Prostration

The diplomatic heart of the mission—the presentation of the President's letter—was both magnificent and humiliating, a carefully staged piece of political theater. Harris, the calm and disciplined mentor, guided Henry through the ritual, instructing him on how to preserve the inviolable dignity of the United States even amid the farce of diplomatic rituals. Every gesture, every measured step, carried weight; every misstep could risk offense.

Henry had the honor, and the burden, of walking between double rows of soldiers, bearing the President's letter to the King of Siam. He felt the hollow irony of it: like the donkey in a fable, he carried a sacred object, receiving accolades meant not for him, but for the relic in his hands. Upon arriving at the Royal Palace, the atmosphere of servitude became absolute. They were ferried in litters past a macabre parade of soldiers—some in tattered European uniforms, others armed with crossbows and gleaming knives—forming a spectacle that seemed lifted from a grotesque stage play. Every detail, from the jeweled uniforms to the silent ranks of prostrate courtiers, was designed to enforce the King's absolute authority.

Inside the audience hall, the effect was overwhelming. The vaulted space pulsed with the silent, bowed forms of a thousand Siamese elite, their faces pressed to the floor. Not one dared meet the King's gaze; even a glance could invite a swift, lethal rebuke. Harris, Henry, and the other foreign officers moved freely in the midst of this sea of submission, maintaining the composure and dignity their nation required. The King, resplendent in a velvet toque ringed with diamonds, sat atop a six-foot throne, an embodiment of divine right. Henry watched, both fascinated and appalled, as even royal brothers and sons groveled in silk robes, their ritualized submission punctuated by the casual puff of a cigar—proof that the Court's ceremonial strictness had its own peculiar eccentricities.

At a precise signal, two immense curtains were drawn with deliberate, thrice-paused motions, concealing the sacred person of His Magnificent Majesty behind heavy folds. It was a final, theatrical flourish, reinforcing both the King's divinity and the subjects' slavish fear. Observing the charade, Henry felt a familiar weariness settle over him. Why, he wondered, must diplomacy demand such an exhausting ballet of prostration and silent threats? Was truth so fragile that it required layers of pomp and the terror of bowed heads? He longed for the honesty of the ocean, for the unvarnished clarity of survival, and questioned whether such ritualized pageantry truly opened doors to understanding—or merely perpetuated a fragile illusion of power.

The Contrast of the Two Worlds

The next day, Harris and Henry had an audience with the Second King, Somdetch Phra Bard Pawarendr Phra Chau Yu Hua. This meeting offered Henry a vision of the potential, and the hypocrisy, of the Asian future.

The Second King, heir-apparent and younger brother of the king, was a man of high culture and intelligence, fluent in English, well-informed on all recent inventions, and possessing a laboratory full of electrical instruments. He received them in a European-style house within his palace grounds, decorated with sofas, mirrors, and a well-stocked library.

Here, the daily farce was put aside. The Second King—commonly known as Prince Pinklao—would greet a stranger like a true gentleman, invite them to sit on European chairs, and pour them tea, while his own son, Prince George Washington, knelt behind him with the royal wives. The Second King demonstrated his modern army, complete with carbines and Zouave bayonets. He was a man who understood the superiority of the West's *science* but was content to maintain his country's *ritual of slavery*.

Henry observed Harris's smooth negotiation. It was easy because the framework was already laid out, and the Siamese—through the highly educated Second King—were eager to modernize *on their own terms*. This ease, however, led Henry to his first significant political insight: the treaties, while opening doors for the United States, offered a slight tangible advantage to the common people of Siam. They served the interests of the King and the royal family, who could now buy more European gadgets and weaponry, while the true slaves—the women, the pariahs—remained bound by the ancient law.

Henry Heusken viewed the Kingdom of Siam as a strictly hierarchical society where universal servitude prevailed, with women occupying the absolute lowest stratum. He characterized Siamese society as an absolute monarchy in which "everything belongs to the King," and whatever the King deemed to ignore passed to the nobility. The entire populace, he observed, existed in a state of mutual bondage: "all are slaves, one to the other." However, Heusken noted, there was an ultimate "caste of pariahs" who were slaves even to the common people: the women.

He highlighted their complete lack of legal rights and their status as economic chattel: Property and Sale: A woman could be sold by her father or her brother. Once married, her husband held total dominion, potentially selling her again if he tired of her.

Domestic Slavery: In her husband's presence, the wife was symbolically and literally subservient, forced to kneel. The husband enjoyed leisure, while the wife was compelled to perform all the labor.

This gendered division of labor was painfully apparent to Heusken in the capital, Bangkok, where he noted that "more than half of the people I saw working were women," particularly on the vital waterways. He recounts witnessing a clear example of this exploitation: a "big fat fellow" lounging and smoking his bourri (Siamese cigar) while two young girls struggled mightily to paddle their boat against the strong current of the Menam River. His visceral reaction—a desire to physically throw the man overboard—was met with a passive shrug from his interpreter, who simply stated, "Costumbres del pais!" (Customs of the country!).

A commercial treaty with a foreign power, such as the one the American mission was attempting to negotiate, would only intensify this economic oppression. The treaty would open Siam to increased international trade and foreign demand for goods and services. Since Siamese men were culturally entitled to leisure and women were forced into nearly all physical and commercial labor, the primary effect of greater trade would be to increase the workload and profitability of the enslaved female workforce, without improving their legal status or share of the profits. The treaty, intended by the West to create economic opportunity, would simply result in the men demanding more work from their wives to exploit the burgeoning foreign markets.

This realization—that diplomacy, even with the best intentions, could be corrupted into a tool for the elite—added a critical layer to Henry's quest. His mission to Japan was not just about opening up a nation, but about ensuring it was opened for the betterment of all, not just the shogunate.

Barbarism and Departure

The final days in Bangkok were a catalogue of Henry's horror and fascination with the country's entrenched cruelties. He witnessed the Menam River—the floating street—become deserted when the King's magnificent gondola, with a thousand oarsmen, passed by, forcing all subjects to flatten themselves against the ground lest they see the royal personage.

Most shocking, however, was the sight of the treatment of the dead. Henry saw the elaborate, months-long preparations for the cremation of a high-ranking priest, only to stumble upon the enclosures for the poor. A body, thrown into the field, was immediately set upon by vultures and dogs that tore at the corpse, fighting for the entrails. The Siamese watched this gruesome, inevitable scene with equanimity.

"Costumbres del pais!" the interpreter shrugged when Henry expressed his nausea and indignation—customs *of the country.*

He was beginning to understand that customs are the deepest roots of a people, far more resistant to change than laws, treaties, or foreign influence. No diplomat could command them to vanish; no treaty could remake them overnight. Diplomacy is never about forcing a society to abandon its rituals or reshape its beliefs, but about navigating these enduring structures with patience and respect. The skill lies in finding a path for cooperation and understanding without attempting to uproot what has been cultivated over generations. Henry realized that opening trade and establishing relations was a matter of accommodation, not imposition, and that the longevity of nations rested on the careful negotiation of their oldest, most stubborn traditions.

The mission to Siam had been successful, concluding with a treaty similar to the British one. The Treaty of Amity, Commerce, and Navigation between the United States and Siam, commonly known as the Harris Treaty, marked a significant milestone in U.S.-Siam relations. Negotiated by Townsend Harris, the first U.S. Consul to Japan, the treaty aimed to establish formal diplomatic and commercial ties between the two nations. It was a revision of the earlier Roberts Treaty of 1833, reflecting the evolving geopolitical landscape and the United States' growing interest in expanding its influence in Asia.

The treaty's provisions included granting the United States most-favored-nation trading status, allowing American merchants to reside and trade freely in designated ports, and ensuring protection under U.S. law for citizens in Siam, while also establishing clear rules for navigation and commerce along Siam's rivers. Importantly, the treaty was framed with mutual respect for Siamese sovereignty and customs, reflecting Harris's careful diplomacy: it opened the kingdom to international trade without imposing foreign authority or undermining traditional governance. By creating a foundation for peaceful commercial and diplomatic relations, the treaty set a precedent for subsequent Western treaties with Siam and demonstrated Harris's skill in balancing American interests with deference to local culture and independence.

Henry, though, described the treaty by noting that the Siam King "did not want to grant us more privileges than the British, we obtained a treaty similar to theirs and left Bangkok."

Regardless, it was a diplomatic triumph for Harris, who was now authorized to go and demand far more from the Tokugawa Shogunate. Henry had received the foundational learning he craved: the protocols, the power dynamics, and a sobering understanding of the thin veneer of civilization.

On May 31, 1856, after a final audience of dismissal with the two Kings, Harris, Henry, and the staff departed. Harris had appointed a temporary American missionary, the Rev. Stephen Mattoon, as Consul, securing the American presence.

As the *San Jacinto* finally set its course for the closed, mythical shores of Japan, Henry carried with him not just maps and diplomatic papers, but a clear, visceral understanding of what he was fighting against: not just geographical isolation, but the barbarism of absolute power. If the world was to be opened, it had to be for the men and women struggling in the dirt, not just for the kings who could afford gold-laminated robes and scientific laboratories.

The true test, the true quest—where precedent and easy manners would count for nothing—was about to begin. The fate of the rising sun awaited.

4

The China Crucible

The *San Jacinto* steamed into Hong Kong on June 12, 1856, and Henry felt the unsettling weight of British colonialism at work. Twelve years prior, this island had been nothing but arid rock and pirate dens. Now, it was a forest of masts, an ordered chaos of streets and handsome, spacious houses, all bent to the supreme task of trade. Even trees, against the laws of nature, had been made to grow.

In the 1850s, Hong Kong was still a young colony, barely a decade old since its cession to Britain after the First Opium War. Perched on a rocky island, it was rapidly transforming from a fishing outpost into a vital trading port. The population numbered around forty thousand, the vast majority Chinese migrants from Guangdong, alongside a small but influential European community of merchants, soldiers, and administrators. The colonial capital, Victoria, stretched along the island's northern shore, facing the harbor, and was divided into wards such as Sheung Wan, Central, and Wan Chai. Queen's Road served as the colony's main artery, lined with warehouses, godowns, and trading houses. On the slopes above, the British built airy bungalows and government offices to escape the heat and disease of the crowded waterfront, while Sheung Wan below was a dense warren of shophouses, markets, and temples.

Victoria Harbour was already a thrumming center of commerce, crowded with clippers, junks, and opium ships moving goods between China and the West. The colony's fortunes rested on this maritime trade—tea, silk, porcelain, and other goods flowing through what was, at its heart, an entrepôt carved from granite and greed. Hong Kong in the 1850s was a place of contrasts: feverish and unfinished, yet already pulsing with the restless ambition that would define its future.

Yet, Henry judged it an abominable town. The air was thick with oppressive heat and a singular avarice. Talk revolved only around business, and venturing outside without the cover of a palanquin—a covered litter carried by four or six bearers—was a risk to one's life due to the heat of the ever-blazing sun. Henry noted that the heat of the Sun of Confucius was an invisible enemy, trapping the pale-skinned inhabitants indoors, forcing them to sit in Chinese armchairs, feet up, smoking Manila cigars and drinking gin and bitters. It was a place of relentless calculation, utterly devoid of the soul or history Henry craved.

The only respite Henry found was in the company of the Dutch Chancellor to Canton, a man named Keep, whom he befriended much as he had other Dutchmen along his journey. Henry later wrote, "Having heard that one of my countrymen was employed in a commercial house and served as Chancellor of the Dutch Consulate in Canton, I went to his office. 'Sir,' I said to him, 'I do not have the honor of your acquaintance, but I have heard that we share the same homeland. I am Mr. So-and-so, and I would be delighted to make your acquaintance.'" Once again, Henry encountered the characteristic hospitality that had so often brightened his travels to Japan.

While staying at Keep's residence, the two enjoyed life as best they could—reclining in Chinese armchairs with their feet up, smoking Manila cigars, and drinking gin and bitters. When the sun dipped toward the horizon, casting its last rays over weary Hong Kong, they would stroll toward the city's own "Champs-Élysées," the Happy Valley. There, seated on a hillside, they let the cool breezes from the bay drift over them.

It was here—amid the manic energy of a trading post carved from granite and greed—that Henry's inner conflict sharpened. He stood at the edge of the East, a young Dutchman remade into an American by ambition, bearing the weight of a grand diplomatic mission. Yet he wondered: could a man who still longed for poetry and the gentle solace of a lady's company truly serve as a bridge between civilizations?

Doubt lingered. Was the world ready for an opening founded on anything nobler than the same ruthless hunger for profit that had built this colony on stone? It was then that Henry resolved to look beyond Hong Kong—to journey deeper into China, to witness for himself the fate of lands long shaped by European conquest.

"My dear man," Henry said to Keep at last, weary of the oppressive heat and the tedium of the port, "I came here to see China—and I believe I must go to Canton."

The Celestial Empire

The journey up the Chou-kieng River to Canton offered Henry his first visceral experience of the true Celestial Empire. Past the Bocca Tigris, where huge, supposedly impregnable Chinese fortresses had fallen to a few British cannon shots during the Opium War—a historical humiliation Henry keenly appreciated—the arid landscape gave way to immense cultivation.

Rice fields, so fresh and verdant they defied description, covered the plains. And then they appeared: the Pagodas. Real Chinese pagodas, with their fanciful shapes and soaring, tiered roofs. It was only then, seeing these structures of an ancient, scornful civilization, that Henry finally grasped his reality: he was really in China, a thousand leagues from the safety of New York or the memory of his mother's farewell in Holland.

Canton itself was a shock. The river was thick with merchant vessels and floating houses, a water-borne city where people were born, lived, and died on the water. But the land was claustrophobic. When Henry arrived, he set out at once for the Dutch Consulate, but the tide was unusually high. Determined to reach it nonetheless, he climbed onto the back of a Chinese porter, who waded with him through the rising water all the way to the building's steps. There, a small crowd quickly gathered—several men clamoring for payment, though only one had actually carried him. Wishing to avoid a scene, Henry paid them all and pressed on, eager to be received by another Dutchman, Van der Hoeven, who had already been informed of his arrival by Keep.

Henry described Canton as a vast and bewildering labyrinth, a city where noise, color, and chaos pressed in from every side. Venturing out with only his sword cane for protection, he traveled by palanquin through narrow lanes where the eaves of opposing roofs seemed to touch. Children trailed behind him, shouting "Fan kwei!"—Foreign Devil—and hurling handfuls of mud. The air was thick with the mingled smells of spice, river water, and decay. Overhead hung painted signboards and banners inscribed with golden characters from Confucius, swaying above a press of merchants, coolies, and porters that filled the crowded streets.

By the 1850s, Canton—known today as Guangzhou—was one of the most populous cities in the world, with close to a million inhabitants packed within its ancient walls. It was still recovering from the Opium War and the recent upheavals of the Taiping Rebellion, its foreign trade tightly controlled despite the Treaty of Nanking's promise of "open ports." Henry observed the city's stark divisions: the walled inner city, guarded by Tartar soldiers and closed to foreigners; the outer suburbs, where immense hongs—the great warehouses of the tea and silk trade—stood filled with the fragrant produce of China, "ready to delight the palates of worthy members of temperance societies." Beyond these quarters lay the foreign factories, a small enclave rebuilt after being destroyed in the war, where European merchants lived in a fragile pocket of order surrounded by the teeming, impenetrable vastness of China.

But the European quarter had its own brand of chaos. Henry noted that here, national pride expressed itself in absurd and often comic forms—most notably in a fierce competition among the foreign powers to see who could raise the tallest flagpole. Each consulate sought to outdo the others, their masts rising higher with every new challenge. In the end, it was the American Consul who triumphed, erecting the loftiest pole of all—only for his government to refuse payment of the fifteen-hundred-dollar bill.

Yet, even in this hostile environment, Henry found moments of wonder. He saw Catholic priests, members of the Society of Foreign Missions, who had adopted the long robes and queues of the Chinese, quietly moving through the city, sacrificing all comfort to bring their gospel. He also met the Turkophone player, a man born in Paris yet traveling the world in a Turkish costume, ready to give concerts. Canton was a crucible of contradictions, preparing Henry for the strange, unsettling hybrid world he knew awaited him in Japan.

The Tomb of Portugal

Henry left Canton in July 1856 for Macao, and the atmosphere changed entirely. The moment he arrived, he felt transported not deeper into China, but into a fragment of old Europe washed up on Asian shores. It was as if he had stepped back into the Iberian world of the 16th century—an empire of faith and fading grandeur.

The Portuguese had established Macao nearly three centuries earlier, in 1557, when the Ming court granted them permission to settle and trade in return for tribute and assistance against pirates. Once the wealthiest port in Asia, it had been the main conduit for silk, porcelain, and silver between China, Japan, and Europe. By the time Henry arrived, however, Macao's glory had dimmed. The rise of Hong Kong after 1842 had drained much of its commerce, leaving behind a languid, nostalgic colony sustained by its churches, mission schools, and the stubborn pride of its people. Still, its cobbled lanes, baroque facades, and shaded plazas spoke of a world more Mediterranean than Chinese—a quiet, melancholy outpost where the Age of Discovery seemed to linger like the scent of incense in a chapel. For Henry, weary from the tumult of Canton, Macao could have felt like an improbable refuge: a piece of Europe dreaming by the South China Sea. Instead, Henry said that Macao was now a "tomb."

He stressed that it was once the jewel of the Portuguese crown, the sole port for trade with China. Now, its harbor was empty of ships, its fortresses crumbling, and its once-wealthy palaces occupied by foreign merchants. The inhabitants, cross-bred with the Chinese and Indians, had fallen, Henry judged, to a lower state than either race.

Everything in Macao spoke of a past greatness that had vanished, leaving only misery and destitution. The one sublime monument to this decay was the ruin of the beautiful Jesuit church, destroyed by fire forty years ago, whose massive front wall alone still stood, defying storms and time. Henry compared its steadfast nobility to that of its former masters, who, though humbled, still maintained themselves with a spirit worthy of admiration.

At the famous Camoens' Cave, where the illustrious poet composed his *Lusiad*, Henry found the sacred place had been ruined by bad taste—an arch and columns erected where nature alone ought to reign.

It was a final, profound lesson on the instability of empire and the transience of human endeavor. He saw a painting in the Cathedral vestry depicting the Portuguese victory over the Dutch in 1622, a victory secured, the sexton claimed, by the miraculous intervention of St. John the Baptist. Henry, a keen skeptic of such religious claims, felt the sting of this long-ago defeat but recognized the Portuguese tenacity.

He penned a bitter verse in the visitors' book, cursing the hands that had profaned the poet's sanctuary. Macao was the warning: the glory of a nation could vanish like the wake of a ship, and only the purity of art or the depth of one's conviction—like the lonely, upright wall of the Jesuit church—could endure.

The Final Call

Henry returned to Hong Kong on July 10, 1856, ready to board the *San Jacinto* and put the continents of confusion and greed behind him.

The anchor was raised, the great frigate set to sail. Then, a disaster occurred when the propeller was discovered to be damaged. The ship was forced to put in at Whampoa, outside of Canton, for repairs, a process that would require a month.

His endurance was tested to the limit. He could not return to the heat of Hong Kong, so he left for Canton to spend the month with Van der Hoeven.

The delay, though frustrating, was beneficial. It forced a final, slow breath, a final reckoning with the world he was leaving. He had seen the best and the worst of the Eastern commercial world; he had understood the power of trade, the shame of slavery, and the hypocrisy of civilized man. He had seen the decay of the old empires and the ruthless rise of the new.

Now, in the heat of August 1856, the final, impatient hour arrived. The propeller was fixed, Harris was aboard, and the *San Jacinto* was finally, irrevocably, pointed northeast.

Henry Heusken, the newly minted U.S. Diplomat, stood on the deck, no longer a mere traveler, but a man armed with the knowledge of human weakness and the unwavering belief in his cause. Before him lay the vast, empty sea, and beyond it, the Land of the Rising Sun, the final, greatest test of his life.

5

Typhoon and the Ethical Test

On August 13, 1856, the final, impatient hour arrived. The propeller of the *San Jacinto* was repaired, the last pungent odors of the Chinese harbors faded behind them, and the massive steam frigate turned her bow toward the heart of the closed world. This was no longer a voyage of curiosity or trade; it was a decisive step into destiny.

Henry stood on deck, feeling the ship creak and groan beneath his feet—a sound that, after months at sea, had become the pulse of his own ambition. The wind shifted, heavy and moody, from pale gray to a bruised, foreboding blue. His mind, sharpened by the philosophical duels of Macao's gardens and the chaotic streets of Canton, turned inward. He was no longer a young adventurer chasing fortune; he was now the appointed vessel of translation and understanding, tasked with a mission never before attempted. Could he, who had felt so solitary amid China's clamoring masses, rise to meet the fierce, uncompromising expectations of Townsend Harris?

Harris, his mentor and a figure of unwavering discipline, stood nearby, his posture rigid against the swell of the sea. To

Harris, the mission was a sacred charge, born of the American spirit of enterprise and liberty. To Henry, it was a profoundly human challenge—an adventure exhilarating and fragile, its success hanging by a slender thread of courage, skill, and endurance.

The Sea's Brutality

Three days into the voyage, on August 16, the fragility of fortune became terrifyingly real.

The waters around the *San Jacinto* were no longer empty. They had become a maritime graveyard, littered with the grim flotsam of a recent, savage typhoon. Chests of tea, great pieces of shattered masts, and the splintered bones of small junks bobbed on the restless waves. Broken spars jutted from the sea like skeletal arms reaching for help, silent reminders of lives and ambitions lost to the wind's cold indifference.

Every fragment was a warning, a memento mori carried across the limitless canvas of the sea. Adventure, Henry scribbled in his journal, was not all glory and discovery; it was risk, isolation, and the quiet knowledge that one wrong wind could undo everything.

Then, amidst the wreckage, a sign of life: a boat was quickly sent toward a section of the mainmast and bamboo that supported a human figure. Soon, the crew carried the poor devil aboard, unable to walk, a Chinese man who had spent forty-eight hours adrift in the frightful predicament. His rescue was a small, blessed triumph of human kindness over the brutality of the elements.

But the sea was not done with them.

Shortly after, a mastless junk appeared, wallowing in the swell. As the *San Jacinto* drew near, the battered vessel erupted in a desperate, frantic noise. The Chinese crew, terrified, beat their gongs and clamored for salvation.

A Lieutenant was dispatched to inquire. He returned with the full measure of the tragedy and the voyage's first true diplomatic dilemma. The Captain of the junk—a man Henry imagined to possess the same stubborn, ancient pride he had witnessed in Canton—refused to abandon his vessel. The crew, however, was in a state of near mutiny, clamoring for rescue.

The Law of the Sea

This was a moral knot only a man of absolute principle could cut. If the Commodore, captain of USS *San Jacinto*, Captain Henry H. Bell received the crew against their captain's will, he would be guilty of aiding and abetting mutiny—a crime against the sacred law of the sea, the immutable code that governed all commercial and military endeavors.

The cries of the drowning men, the frantic beating of the gongs, echoed across the water, assaulting Henry's ears. He felt a profound, aching urge to intervene, to defy the sterile, rigid Law in favor of simple, immediate Mercy.

But Harris's gaze was fixed on the horizon, unwavering. He was a Plain Truth man, and his truth was anchored in order.

The Commodore, backed by Harris's silent, unyielding sanction, made the dreadful decision: he would not interfere in the affairs of another ship's captain. The *San Jacinto* steamed away from the dismasted junk. The cries of the despairing sailors, their frantic signals of distress, echoed in Henry's ears until the distance swallowed the miserable vessel.

It was a cold, necessary lesson administered by the Commodore and his mentor without a single word. Diplomacy was not always kindness. It often demanded the rigorous, painful defense of principle, even at the cost of human life. The grand mission to Japan was not just about idealism; it was about unyielding, hard-edged Western Law.

The Final Approach

The test was immediately followed by a desperate act of charity.

Two more dismasted junks appeared in the distance. To the first, they were able to offer aid—a spare sail, a mast, and some rigging—a slight reprieve from the typhoon's wrath.

The second vessel was in a far worse state. Armed with a ton cannon, which it fired repeatedly in distress signals, its captain finally admitted that the junk was taking water fast. Seeing the obvious and inescapable danger, the Commodore finally agreed to take the entire company aboard. This time, their own captain did not object—he, too, recognized that the situation had grown desperate, and that abandoning their ship was the only course left.

However, the conditions set by the Commodore were sharp and final: only a parcel of their own clothes could be brought. The abandoned vessel was to be set afire. The Captain, a dog, a cat, and fifty-three Chinese sailors climbed aboard the American frigate—a sudden, chaotic influx of foreign desperation onto the disciplined decks of the warship.

A lieutenant was sent to ignite the junk, the ultimate declaration of abandonment and mercy. They watched, their eyes fixed on the dark shadow of the vessel as the sun dipped into the ocean. Yet, contrary to all expectations, the fire never erupted. The doomed junk, a silent testament to the sea's power, simply drifted on, untouched by the flames of finality.

That night, after assisting a Siamese junk by giving them water, the *San Jacinto* sailed on, the rescued Chinese clustered below deck, their fate now woven into the tapestry of the American mission.

The sea was empty now. The chaos of China, the corruption of Macao, and the ethical compromises of the ocean were behind them. Ahead, the vast silence of the Pacific and then Japan.

Days later, the sky cleared, and the sea turned a deep, expectant blue. It was then that they saw Japan.

Henry Heusken, the young man who had journeyed for a year to find his purpose, saw the distant shores rise from the horizon, black, mysterious, and utterly silent. He had shed the baggage of the West. He felt the cold, hard knowledge that soon isolation would settle upon him on those shores.

He was no longer sailing toward a dream. He was sailing toward his destiny, toward the great, impossible barrier that only his voice, his mind, and his singular courage could hope to breach.

6

The Barrier of Shimoda

The mountains of Cape Idzu rose from the sea, a chain of black, sharp teeth guarding the secrets of a nation. On August 21, 1856, the *San Jacinto* dropped anchor in the tranquil but deeply unwelcoming waters of Shimoda Bay.

Shimoda was one of the first two Japanese ports opened to American trade under the Convention of Kanagawa (1854), following Commodore Matthew Perry's expedition. Before this, it had been an insular town, rarely touched by foreign influence. The bay was a small harbor on the southeastern coast of Japan's Izu Peninsula. Naturally sheltered, the crescent-shaped bay offered calm waters ideal for anchorage for a few ships, with hills and cliffs rising steeply behind the town, dotted with forests and occasional rice paddies. The town of Shimoda stretched along the waterfront, a cluster of wooden houses, warehouses, and narrow docks squeezed between the hills and the water. Streets wound irregularly through the settlement, following the contours of the land, and life was quiet and orderly, centered around fishing, farming, small markets, temples, and shrines. The surrounding coastline was rugged, making the harbor a prized safe haven for ships navigating the stormy stretch of the Pacific.

Even though Shimoda was a small, secluded harbor tucked away at the southern tip of the Izu Peninsula, it offered clear advantages over the other port that Commodore Matthew C. Perry had secured under the Treaty of Kanagawa. The alternative, Hakodate—situated far to the north on the island of Hokkaido—was remote and less practical for regular contact with the heart of Japan's political power. By contrast, Shimoda's proximity to Edo, modern-day Tokyo, made it a strategic choice. It placed American representatives within easier reach of the shogun's government and the center of decision-making.

For Henry Heusken, the sight of Japan was the climax of a journey that had spanned continents, oceans, and moral reckonings. He was here, at the heart of the great isolation, the point where the West's inevitable tide met the East's immovable rock.

As the U.S. warship pulled into the bay and even before the formalities could even begin, a boat approached, carrying the Shimoda Governor's secretary and two figures Henry scrutinized with professional intensity: Dutch interpreters, he thought. The language of his homeland, the very currency of his value, was the only key permitted to unlock this kingdom. The two men, Toko Juro and his colleague, were the first links in the chain of Japanese power, their very presence confirming Henry as the chosen conduit for all interaction.

Harris, ever the consummate diplomat, immediately dispatched a letter written by Henry notifying the Governors of Shimoda—known as the Goyosho—of his imminent arrival. The response came swiftly, but it was tinged with a carefully measured suspicion. The Goyosho would receive the Consul-General, they declared, yet they could not refrain from asking a pointed, almost provocative question: which held higher rank, the Consul-General or the Commodore? The inquiry was subtle but loaded, a test of American intentions and an assertion of Japanese protocol and pride.

Henry, working closely with Harris, helped craft the reply with painstaking care. Their answer was precise: the ranks were entirely different, operating in separate spheres of authority. Harris, they explained, represented the United States as a diplomat, tasked with law, negotiation, and the enforcement of treaty obligations. The Commodore, by contrast, commanded the naval forces, wielding military power rather than legal or diplomatic authority. The distinction was delicate but essential. The presence of the frigate, while secondary to Harris's office, served as a silent yet undeniable guarantor of his authority—a subtle reminder that the law he represented carried the weight not only of treaties, but of the nation behind them.

The Political Earthquake

Eventually, once the formal exchange of letters had ended, Harris and Henry went ashore, where Japanese officials received them, accompanied by officers and an escort of soldiers. The reception was polite, even ceremonious: the officials offered compliments, bowed deeply, and expressed delight at the Consul's good health. Yet their courtesy was a thin veil over palpable unease.

Henry could sense the tension beneath the ritual gestures, the nervous formality of a nation newly forced into contact with the outside world. He understood that the challenge before them was immense, one that required more than diplomacy—it demanded an understanding of the political earthquake that had shaken the Tokugawa Shogunate during the three turbulent years since Japan's gates had first been pried open, but this would be the first time an American would be there permanently.

When Commodore Perry first sailed into Edo Bay in 1853, Japan's rulers were caught utterly unprepared. The Tokugawa Shogunate had no actual foreign policy, no coherent strategy for confronting the expanding powers of the West. For years, Dutch and Chinese traders had warned of Europe's growing dominance in Asia—of China's humiliation in the Opium Wars and the gunboat diplomacy that followed—but those warnings had been met with denial. The Shogunate clung to its centuries-old isolation, a regime surviving on inertia, believing that if Japan sealed itself off tightly enough, the tides of history might simply wash around it.

In their panic, the Tokugawa authorities committed what many would later see as a fatal breach of custom: they broke with centuries of precedent by consulting outside their own tight circle. Perry's demands were circulated among the feudal lords—the daimyō—including those long excluded from the central government. This act, a desperate attempt to share responsibility, was in fact a confession of weakness. It ignited political chaos. The daimyō, many of whom had grown resentful of their reduced power under the Shogunate, seized the chance to voice their own opinions on foreign affairs. What began as a debate over how to handle foreign ships quickly transformed into a national reckoning over who had the right to rule Japan.

Old enemies of the Tokugawa saw their opportunity. From the Imperial Court in Kyoto came new whispers of opposition, carefully fanned by factions hostile to the Shogunate. Perry's arrival had been explained away as an unavoidable concession to "humanity," but the mission of Townsend Harris—demanding residence, legal rights, and open commerce—was something far more dangerous. His presence threatened not just Japan's isolation, but the very foundations of the feudal order itself. Thus, when Harris and Henry arrived at Shimoda, they had not merely stepped ashore in a quiet fishing port—they had entered a nation on the brink of revolution, a civil war waged not with armies, but with petitions, ceremony, and the invisible weapons of pride and tradition.

The War of Compliments

The audience at the *Goyosho* upon arrival in the bay and after the letters was a subtle, prolonged battle of wills. After pipes, tobacco, and the delivery of dinner—soups, fish, duck, and eggs served in lacquered wooden cups—the niceties ended.

The Governors launched their offensive. A flood and an earthquake had struck them, they explained, and the whole country was in a state of disarray.

In consequence, they would be delighted if His Excellency, the Consul-General, would be so kind as to leave and come back in a year or two.

Harris, the relentless man of principle, did not blink. He answered simply that he could do nothing of the kind. He had orders from his government to obey. He was in Japan to stay.

The debate continued, fueled by the Governors' intense aversion to having a Consul on their territory. They challenged the necessity of his presence, arguing that the treaty merely *permitted* an appointment and that they, the Japanese, could take care of wrecked sailors and American interests. Henry, translating the measured, hard edge of Harris's responses, felt the tension rise. The Governors were determined to persevere in the system of isolation that had defined their world for three centuries.

After prolonged, exhausting debate, the Governors conceded: they would offer Harris one of the Buddhist Temples of Shimoda or Kakizaki, since no house was ready, to serve as his residence and the first U.S. consulate to Japan.

In the 1850s, it was common in Japan for travelers and guests—including samurai, merchants, pilgrims, and, later, foreigners—to be lodged in Buddhist temples. Many temples maintained guest quarters known as shukubō, offering orderly but straightforward accommodations of tatami rooms, sliding doors, and paper lanterns. These temples served as both places of rest and of quiet reflection, scattered along major routes and in provincial towns. When Henry arrived in Japan, such temples functioned as an essential part of the country's travel infrastructure, providing safety, food, and shelter in a society where inns were few and travel was tightly regulated.

Even as they were discussing their housing, the Japanese made a final attempt to rid themselves of their "dear, dear friend, the Consul-General," who came during a second visit by the governors to the ship. The Governors, in a calculated move, turned directly to the Commodore of the *San Jacinto* and asked him in the most *naïve* manner if he would not simply take the Consul-General with him and return to the United States.

The Commodore, a military man, delivered the final, crushing blow to their hopes. He, too, was bound by orders and had been commanded to leave the Consul-General at Shimoda. The final attempt had failed. The Governors, at a loss, simply reverted to etiquette, offering presents of half a large fish and a pair of chickens to the officers—a gift Henry recorded as a final, petty diplomatic insult.

Diplomatic gift-giving was a standard practice during this era, and Harris and Henry fully intended to use this tradition to their advantage. They brought numerous gifts to Japan to gain favor with high-ranking officials and demonstrate the quality of American craftsmanship. These included items of considerable value and intrigue, such as liquor and even three Colt revolvers.

In the context of these significant diplomatic offerings, the meager presentation of a fish and some chickens by the Japanese was therefore regarded by Henry as an almost insulting, or at least insignificant, gesture that barely registered as a diplomatic gift.

The Temple Becomes a Prison

The agreed-upon residence was Gyokusenji Temple (Jocsenji). But during Henry's inspection of his new workplace and home, the Japanese revealed the true nature of their hospitality. They needed to reserve two or three rooms for Japanese officers who would serve as an honor guard—protecting the foreigners from the people's insults, and, incidentally, executing any orders the Consul might have.

Henry understood the unspoken truth immediately: the temple was to be their prison, and the "helpful officers," their wardens, were placed there to observe every slightest movement. It was a perfect recreation of the Dutch trading post of Deshima.

Deshima was a small, fan-shaped artificial island in Nagasaki Bay, no more than a few hundred feet across, and for over two centuries, it served as the Dutch Empire's gilded prison in Japan. Built in the 1630s as part of the Tokugawa Shogunate's sakoku—or "closed country"—policy, it was designed to wall off Western influence while still permitting a tightly controlled trickle of trade. The Dutch were Japan's only sanctioned European partners. Yet, they lived under constant surveillance: confined behind high walls, forbidden to bring families, practice Christianity, or freely walk the streets of Nagasaki. Every transaction, conversation, and movement was monitored by Japanese officials.

Once or twice a year, the Dutch chief trader was allowed to travel to Edo to pay homage to the shogun—a ritual of submission that underscored their captivity. From the mainland, Deshima appeared almost like a floating curiosity. But for those trapped within it, the island was both a bridge and a barrier—a place where East and West met under the watchful eye of a nation determined to remain untouched.

Harris, though grateful for their "attention," firmly refused to have the spy-guards within his living quarters. However, to avoid appearing too difficult from the outset, he compromised: a small house in the temple court would be perfectly suitable for the two officers, where they would be "day and night, at our disposal." The Governor had won the presence of the wardens; Harris had secured the private space of the Legation itself.

The arrangement was emblematic of the Tokugawa government's delicate balancing act: fulfilling its new diplomatic obligations while keeping the foreign presence strictly confined. Placing the Americans in a temple became symbols of Japan's uneasy first contact with the outside world—at once sanctuaries and subtle prisons.

On September 3, 1856, Harris ordered a defiant act of U.S. sovereignty at the temple: the crew of the *San Jacinto* erected a mast in the temple court and hoisted the American flag without the slightest opposition from the Japanese government. It was the first time the Stars and Stripes had been raised in Japan as a symbol of permanent diplomatic residence.

That day, Henry stood and watched as the *San Jacinto* raised its anchor and slipped slowly from view. Climbing a nearby hill, he caught one final glimpse of the ship before it disappeared beyond the horizon—"the last object that still linked me to the Western world." The long voyage was over. He had arrived at his diplomatic post, surrounded by the vast, silent, and at times hostile majesty of Japan.

He was not entirely alone in his new destiny. His mentor, Townsend Harris, was by his side, along with four Chinese servants whom Harris had hired in China: a cook and his assistant, a tailor, and a washman. Beyond their small household, the Japanese authorities had stationed a detachment of soldiers within the new consulate—guards whose true purpose was unmistakable. They were there not only to protect but to watch, serving as both sentinels and spies over every movement within the American compound.

Thus began the great struggle—not merely for diplomatic recognition, but for the soul of a nation poised on the threshold between isolation and the modern world.

7

The Monastic Siege

The silence was the enemy. After the great symphony of the sea and the markets of China, the isolated compound of the Gyokusenji Temple at Shimoda was a vault of profound, suffocating quiet.

Townsend Harris and Henry Heusken were alone—two fragments of the West stranded between the vast, unchanging ocean and the mountains of Idzu. The local authorities, with their meticulous spy-guards posted in the courtyard, had achieved their objective: the American consulate was, effectively, a monastic prison. No messages arrived, and the deliberate, baffling pace of Japanese life seemed to exist only to test the limits of Western sanity.

Harris, the stoic Puritan, found solace in the meticulous order of his work, taking careful notes on the strange, elegant customs of the people who watched him with cautious curiosity. Harris also started taking long walks to areas he seemed to be permitted to explore, but never strayed too far from their temple consulate. But for Henry, the young man whose soul craved light and movement, the monotonous life was a constant struggle.

Yet, slowly, something unexpected took root—a growing affection for the place itself. The air was clean, the landscape breathtaking, the people disciplined yet graceful. Henry found himself exploring the surrounding countryside within the imposed limits, sketching the rocky coastlines and attempting hesitant smiles with villagers who seemed both wary and amused by the fair-haired foreigner. He realized they were poised between wonder and uncertainty, part of an extraordinary, fragile beginning.

The Unbroken Spirit

Their internal world, however, was immediately shattered by Japan's external fury.

On September 21, 1856, a frightful hurricane laid waste to the coast. All the junks in the bay were cast against the shore, and almost a third of Shimoda town was destroyed. When Henry surveyed the carnage the next morning—masts scattered on the beach, debris of ships and houses—he witnessed the true, unbreakable core of the Japanese spirit.

Not a cry of despair was heard. Not even sorrow was visible on their faces. On the contrary, they seemed quite indifferent to the tempest, already busy repairing the damage with a quiet, unhurried intensity. It was a stoicism that shamed the emotional, volatile West, a terrifying self-possession that Harris admired but knew would be an immense obstacle to their diplomatic mission.

Seizing the moment, Harris recognized that their mission could not wait for the Shogun's convenience. The silence had to be broken by a clear declaration of authority. On September 25, 1856, Harris, with Henry's help, penned a letter to the Japanese Minister of Foreign Affairs: he was no mere Consul, but an Ambassador with full powers, the bearer of a letter from the President to the Emperor. Consequently, he intended to go to Edo, the Capital known today as Tokyo, where he himself needed to present the letter.

This bold move was the first thrust in their siege, a deliberate violation of the quiet protocols designed to trap them.

Electric Shocks of Contact

As Harris and Henry waited for permission to travel to Edo and deliver the President's letter, their monotonous life was occasionally interrupted by sudden, electric shocks from the outside world—reminders that they had not been entirely forgotten.

On September 30, 1856, the Dutch corvette *Medusa*, under Captain Fabius, cast anchor in the bay. The sight of the flag of Henry's native country was a powerful and heartbreaking antidote to his isolation. Welcomed warmly by the officers, Henry found comfort in their company, in familiar language and shared memories. For three days, the temple felt less like a prison. But Captain Fabius, having seen the devastation left by a recent hurricane and judging the harbor unsafe, hastened his departure. When the *Medusa* sailed away, she left behind a deep void in Henry's heart.

The visits continued. In October, the American schooner *General Pierce* arrived—a symbol of commerce—but her cargo of rifles was rejected as "too old," a small commercial failure that underscored Japan's cautious approach to modernization.

The most welcome interruption came on November 12, 1856, with the arrival of the Russian corvette *Olivuzza*, commanded by Captain Constantin Possiet, who brought a ratified treaty between Russia and Japan that offered Russia similar style port access as the United State. However, at this juncture, Russia had no intention of stationing a Consul General alongside Harris and Heusken in Shimoda. For the Russians, the arrival was merely a transient visit to the port, and none of their party intended to remain behind. Henry found the Russian officers—charming, courteous, and well-bred—to be a delightful respite from isolation, and their company helped him and Harris pass the final weeks of November and December more pleasantly. They were all engaged in the same diplomatic struggle, and camaraderie bridged the distance between nations.

Yet the Japanese government soon reminded them of its vigilance. Every letter received by the Russian officers through Nagasaki had been opened and read—proof that European powers did not hold a monopoly on such indignities. The watchful wardens stationed in the consulate courtyard were, in miniature, an embodiment of the national policy of unrelenting suspicion.

That same vigilance occasionally exposed troubles within the Consulate itself. In November, two of the Chinese servants brought to Shimoda by Harris were reported to have ventured into town in search of opium, and apparently succeeded in obtaining some. The Japanese authorities promptly informed Harris, who immediately confronted the two men and demanded that they surrender the contraband. After some reluctance, they complied and returned the opium.

Even so, the closing days of the year were not without tension. On Tuesday, December 23, 1856, Henry went out walking alone and unarmed. Along the road, he encountered a Japanese man wearing a coat of arms on his sleeve, though Henry could not discern whose. As soon as the man saw him, he brandished a long stick menacingly, then drew his sword. Henry stopped short and, realizing he was defenseless, turned back toward the Consulate. When he reported the incident, Harris sharply instructed him, "Never to go out unarmed again."

It was the only instance in 1856 when any Japanese had threatened them, an incident as curious as it was isolated. The authorities investigated, but without a clear identification of the crest, the swordsman remained unknown and unaccountable for his actions. One might wonder, though—had Henry carried the sword-cane he had brought with him while going around cities in China, would he ever have stood a chance against a samurai?

Samurai training was a lifelong process that began in childhood and was rooted in the philosophy of Bushidō ("The Way of the Warrior"), emphasizing loyalty, honor, and self-discipline. While much of their time was spent on administrative duties, formal training continued at martial arts schools (dōjō) that focused on swordsmanship (especially kenjutsu), archery (kyūdō), and, often, jūjutsu (unarmed combat).

Education was highly valued; a samurai was expected to be literate and knowledgeable in classical Chinese and Japanese literature, alongside military strategy. Within society, the samurai were responsible for maintaining order and were the ultimate moral and political authority. They dictated law, collected taxes, and enforced the Shogun's will.

The Samurai in 1850s Japan were not the dynamic, constantly warring soldiers of earlier centuries, but rather a declining, hereditary ruling class and bureaucratic elite within the rigid Tokugawa Shogunate. Membership in the samurai class was almost entirely determined by birth, not by merit or individual accomplishment.

They constituted about six to seven percent of the population and sat atop the rigid four-tier social hierarchy (Shi-Nō-Kō-Shō—Samurai, Peasants, Artisans, Merchants). While they theoretically held the exclusive right to carry the daishō (the long and short swords), most samurai had become civil administrators, tax collectors, or police officials rather than active warriors, living on stipends (kokudaka) paid by their feudal lords (daimyō).

Despite their privileged position, many low-ranking samurai were poor, indebted, and deeply dissatisfied with the Shogunate's stagnation, making them particularly receptive to radical, anti-foreign ideologies.

The Holiday Season

The holiday season found Henry and Townsend Harris far from home, passing Christmas and New Year's in a distant land. Instead of the warmth of family gatherings or the cheer of bustling streets, they faced quiet days marked by illness and isolation. Harris, weakened and unwell, spent much of this period confined and reflective, while Henry, his assistant and only real companion, did what he could to keep their small household in order. The festive sounds of home were replaced by the stillness of Japan's winter air. For two men accustomed to movement and purpose, it was a heavy kind of stillness—one that pressed against their spirits.

The loneliness of the season was unmistakable. Both men had grown used to a life abroad, yet the holidays sharpened their sense of distance. Harris noted in his journal that it had been years since he had spent Christmas among friends and family in New York. By his count, eight Christmases had now passed in foreign lands—from the coasts of Asia to the courts of Siam. Henry, by contrast, was still new to this rhythm of wandering. The previous Christmas had found him at sea, bound for the Cape of Good Hope, and though that journey was adventurous, it lacked the profound solitude that this year brought.

When New Year's Day arrived, the feeling of isolation did not lift. Harris, still weakened, found himself daydreaming of walking the familiar streets of New York—calling on loved ones, exchanging greetings, and watching the city wake to another year. But in Shimoda, there were no such scenes to comfort him. The only people to whom he could offer a "Happy New Year" were Henry and a few Chinese servants—men for whom this day carried no special meaning. The contrast between what was and what might have been hung heavily over him.

Yet even amid their melancholy, both men could not help but reflect on how momentous the year 1856 had been. They had traveled across the world, visited dozens of ports and cities, and played their part in the shaping of new relations between nations. Together, they had helped secure the treaty with Siam, an achievement that would stand as one of the highlights of their mission. The year had been full of motion, accomplishment, and historic significance—but its end found them weary and low in spirit.

For Harris, his diplomatic mission in Japan had moved painfully slowly, testing both his patience and his confidence. The cultural barriers, the cautious evasions of the Japanese officials, and the long months of waiting had all taken their toll. To be ill, lonely, and uncertain of progress was a hard combination for a man of his resolve. He confessed that the isolation gnawed at him more than he had expected, and that the lack of success weighed heavier than any physical ailment.

But Harris was in poor health during this time. In early January, he noted that since the previous April, he had been "wasting away in flesh," having lost a total of forty pounds. Desperate to recover, he experimented with various remedies and adjusted his diet in hopes of regaining his strength, but nothing seemed to bring relief. Determined to improve his condition, he even incorporated regular exercise into his routine, walking five to six miles a day around Shimoda. Despite these efforts, his health continued to decline—a slow, relentless deterioration that reflected both the physical strain of his mission and the isolation of his circumstances.

Still, Harris and Henry did not surrender to despair. As the final hours of 1856 faded, they made a quiet resolution to endure with renewed determination. "We must keep up our spirits and hope for the best," Harris wrote, capturing both his fatigue and his stubborn faith. The New Year began not with celebration but with resolve—a recognition that though they were far from home and far from comfort, their work still mattered. In the long silence of that winter, two weary men looked toward the uncertain promise of another year, clinging to the belief that perseverance would yet bring reward.

The Crane and the Compromise

The Japanese government's response to Harris's escalation from months of hounding came on February 22, 1857. Having fired a salute in honor of Washington's birthday—a small, necessary act of protocol—Henry learned the painful truth: Edo does not want to enter into direct negotiations with Harris. The Governors of Shimoda possessed full powers to act themselves.

Harris's patience, vast though it was, began to fray. Letters to Edo went unanswered, and audiences were endlessly delayed. They were stranded envoys in a quiet harbor.

However, to mitigate this refusal, the Governor presented a concession: an unheard-of invitation to visit him in his private home, rather than the cold, official *Goyosho*. This was a break in protocol, a subtle admission that Harris was a personage who could not be ignored indefinitely.

On February 23, 1857, Henry and Harris were carried to the Governor's home in Norimons. A norimon (or norimono) was a type of enclosed palanquin used in Japan, especially during the Edo period (1603-1868), for transporting high-ranking individuals such as samurai, officials, and nobles. It was essentially a portable carriage carried on poles by bearers, allowing the occupant to travel in relative comfort and privacy while remaining elevated above the crowded streets. However, Henry just noted that they are "such exceedingly short litters," so much so that he did not know what to do with his legs. The Japanese bent their own backs under their bodies, a wonderful custom Henry could not emulate due to his Western, tight-fitting clothes.

Freed from his uncomfortable confines upon arrival at the Governor's house, Henry observed the austerity of the high-ranking officials. The rooms in the Governor's house were basically identical to any Shimoda shopkeeper's house: matting on the floor, paper instead of panes at the windows, and no furniture save the two benches built expressly for their foreign legs.

The dinner was a parade of more than twelve entrees, filled with symbolic significance. A huge dish was presented bearing a tree whose branches held cranes carved from radishes, a compliment that symbolized longevity. The First Governor then performed the most incredible compliment: he made tea with his own hands, explaining the process with the pride of an amateur, warming the tea, boiling the water, and presenting the delicate service to his "close friend, the Consul-General."

Then came the ritual of the sake (rice wine). The Governor drank to Henry's health, and Henry, to his palate's torment, had to reciprocate, keeping a pleasant countenance as the detestable liquor burned its way to his stomach. He was rewarded with a beautiful porcelain cup for each health offering, but his discomfort was immense. Henry hated sake.

Henry observed a deeper, profound isolation at the Governor's residence: the total lack of women. High Imperial officers were compelled to live as bachelors, their wives deliberately left as hostages in Edo, and concubines strictly forbidden by stern laws, lest the "poor enchanting sex" inadvertently betray state secrets. This enforced absence of a "man's angel of mercy" lent a palpable emptiness and a certain sadness to the Governor's dinner table, confirming Henry's view of the Shogunate as a paranoid, cruel regime.

The cruelty was mirrored in the rigid structure of daily Japanese life. In the 1850s, women existed within a fiercely hierarchical and patriarchal society, deeply influenced by Confucian principles. Their principal roles were those of obedient daughters, devoted wives, and nurturing mothers. While women of all classes were expected to serve and support their families, they were consistently regarded as subordinate to men and excluded from political and educational opportunities. Upper-class women faced the severest social constraints, enduring early arranged marriages and limited public presence. In contrast, peasant women gained a degree of autonomy by working alongside men in the fields. Regardless of class, a woman's value was chiefly measured by her conformity to ideals of obedience, diligence, and self-sacrifice.

The dinner itself, despite the somber atmosphere, represented a quiet victory of patience—a softening of the outer shell of Japanese resistance. Harris had been firmly rebuffed on the critical issue of moving to Edo, but he had successfully forced a genuine cultural concession from the officials. The tide was undeniably turning, but its progress was agonizingly slow, measured in the gentle sway of norimon (palanquin) rides and the bitter taste of cups of rice wine. Though they were still far from the Shogun's heart, Henry Heusken knew, with a certainty that burned like the detestable sake, that he was inexorably inching closer to his destiny.

8

The War of Politeness

On February 25, 1857, the siege ended, and the war began. The battlefield was not the open sea, nor the fortified gate of a city, but a modest, mat-floored room in the *Goyosho*, the Governor's headquarters. After dinner, Henry and Harris were finally engaged in official interviews with the representatives of the Shogunate. For Henry, the young linguist who was the vital link in every exchange, these early exchanges were both a fascination and an exquisite torture.

The Japanese officials, led by Governors Inoue (Prince of Shinano) and Okada (Prince of Bingo), spoke in an endless series of polished circles. Answers were so polite, so refined, that Henry, translating their phrases, found himself constantly searching for the rock of meaning beneath the vast, rolling surface of ambiguity. Promises dissolved into delicate *maybes*; refusals came wrapped in layers of ceremonial smiles.

It was diplomacy as a dance of shadows, a strategy rooted in patience and harmony, designed to wear down the Western passion for confrontation. Henry watched Harris, whose calm persistence anchored every meeting, and began to understand that success here would not come from pressure or argument, but from endurance. They were taking baby steps, but they were steps forward nonetheless—small, crucial victories that the Japanese, so isolated, regarded as vast concessions.

The System of Mutual Spying

In the quiet hours between these agonizing meetings, Henry tracked the full measure of the system built to contain and control them.

First, there was the constant, smothering surveillance. Initially, Henry could not step outside the consulate without a *go-bangoshi*, a police officer, dogging his steps like his own shadow. The government claimed these guards were for their protection against the populace—a "guard of honor." But Henry knew the truth: the poor populace of Japan was so rigorously restrained that they dared not look at the foreigners. Women, especially the young girls, fled at a gallop at their approach, running as though the "enemy of mankind was at their heels." Even the dogs of Shimoda mistook them for a "heavenly orb," raising a frightful alarm whenever the "Foreign Devils" appeared, while only the aloof cats seemed to ignore the rigorous laws against the West.

Secondly, the little house in the consulate yard was a spy satellite, perpetually occupied by two officers relieved daily, ensuring a constant, fresh pair of eyes.

Thirdly, during official visits, Harris and Henry were flanked by half a dozen Japanese secretaries who wrote down every single word uttered. This insult was reinforced by the presence of three imperial spies in Shimoda, accredited by Edo, who were empowered to attend all conferences and enter the Governor's house at any moment, even at night. Henry saw that every Japanese spies on another, a necessary evil of absolute rule.

In addition to spying, other tactics were used against Harris and Henry. The Governors of Shimoda were so deeply ensnared in the rigid web of Tokugawa protocol that they refused to respond to any of Harris's letters in writing. Every communication that Henry painstakingly drafted in Dutch on Harris's behalf was met only with verbal replies. This allowed the Governors to maintain maximum deniability and flexibility: nothing was formally recorded, nothing could be cited against them later, and they could adjust their position at a moment's notice without breaking protocol.

Harris, frustrated by the evasions, repeatedly protested, insisting that these were official diplomatic communications and demanded proper, written responses. He argued that a verbal exchange was insufficient for matters of law, commerce, and treaty obligations. Yet, his complaints were met with polite persistence, as the Governors carefully balanced courtesy with caution. For Henry, serving as scribe and translator, the situation was a constant exercise in patience and tact, navigating a system where the very act of writing carried political weight, and where ink on paper could be treated as dangerously binding.

Harris's Ultimatum

The accumulation of these small indignities finally drove Harris, the man of "Plain Truth," to a dramatic, necessary confrontation. He realized his gentle, courteous remonstrances were useless against such an immovable, tenacious bureaucracy.

One fine day, the calm, disciplined diplomat transformed into the furious representative of a sovereign power. Henry, translating the blistering, unvarnished Dutch, felt the tension snap in the room.

Harris boldly addressed the Governors: he declared that his government would never tolerate such outrages against the person of its representative, a figure whose sacred diplomatic character was recognized by *all civilized nations*. By concluding treaties, Japan had subjected itself to the general laws of nations, and Harris flatly refused to be held responsible for the indignation and reprisals Japan was drawing upon itself.

"I demand," Harris stated, his voice ringing with absolute authority, "that the guards posted at the door of the consulate and who treat like a prisoner a representative of the United States be immediately removed, or I shall declare myself a prisoner, and you will have to take the consequences."

The speech struck home. It was not a plea, but an ultimatum based on the Law of Nations. When Harris and Henry returned to the consulate, the guards were already packing. By sunset, the courtyard was empty, and only Harris, Henry, and their servants who were directly attached to the Legation remained.

The victory was swift and absolute. Harris also declared that he would no longer receive any dignitary flanked by secretaries who intended to insult him by recording every word, and the very next time he saw a spy, he would eject him. Since that day, the spies and secretaries vanished from the Consulate. However, Henry knew that secret surveillance continued, with secretaries likely hidden behind the thin partitions of the *Goyosho*, but appearances were saved, and a significant diplomatic right had been secured.

The Skirmish over Silver

With the issue of security momentarily settled, the negotiation shifted to the bedrock of all foreign relations: money.

The Governors, tenacious and commercially shrewd, had an outrageously unfair stance on currency. In the 1850s, the world of currency was a chaotic patchwork, with each nation—or even region—minting its own coins, often of wildly differing weight, purity, and value. Silver and gold dominated international trade, but the exact standard of a "dollar" or its equivalent could vary dramatically depending on where one stood. In Japan, the situation was particularly vexing. The Japanese silver ichibu (or Ichibugin, Ichibukin), a small, rectangular, bar-shaped coin that was a key part of Japan's currency system during the Edo period, weighed less than an American silver dollar. By strict calculation, three ichibu together were worth less than a single U.S. dollar. Yet the Japanese insisted, for the purposes of foreign trade, that one American dollar be treated as equal to only one ichibu.

For Harris, Henry, and the American merchants navigating these financial shoals, the practical effect was staggering. The Americans were effectively paying more than three times the actual value of the goods they purchased, a silent tax imposed not by law but by the rigid conventions of a currency system foreign to them. This discrepancy was not unique to Japan; in the 1850s, traders from Britain to China faced similar confusions, as coins from different empires, colonies, and local mints circulated simultaneously.

Yet in Japan, where foreign access was tightly controlled, and the Shogunate's rules were enforced with ritualistic precision, the misalignment of value was as much a tool of control as a quirk of economics. Every exchange carried not just financial implications, but subtle lessons in authority, hierarchy, and the delicate dance required for Americans to conduct trade in a land that measured wealth—and compliance—differently from anywhere else in the world.

The Japanese argument was based on their absolute monarchy. All gold and silver in the mine had the same value as "wood or stone." Its worth was acquired only when the government minted it with its stamp. Therefore, all foreign money had to be melted and re-minted into *ichibus*.

Harris, the former New York merchant, was incandescent. Henry translated his precise arguments: all civilized nations gave foreign minted silver its accurate rate of exchange and did not charge for melting expenses. Thus, Harris had Henry let everyone know that the U.S. would refuse to pay for anything until the dollar was accepted at its just value.

It was only through such firm, logical arguments that the Japanese began to yield. They finally agreed to Harris's proposal to weigh silver against silver, but they stubbornly demanded a 25% fee for minting expenses. Harris countered that such expenses in other countries were only one-half of one percent, and threatened to bring American craftsmen to handle the minting for one percent.

The Japanese, forced to recognize the blatant unfairness of their demand, finally came down to six percent. The currency question, the foundation of all future trade, was amicably, if grudgingly, settled.

The Cracks in the Wall

By March 1857, the tiny American legation in Shimoda had achieved a series of remarkable symbolic and practical victories. They had won the abolition of public surveillance, allowing them to move and meet without the constant scrutiny of Japanese officials. They gained the right to meet government officers privately, without Japanese secretaries present, and they had successfully resolved the vexing currency crisis, ensuring fairer trade terms for American merchants.

Beyond these immediate successes, the legation secured principles of far-reaching importance. They established that the port of Nagasaki, previously open to Russian vessels, would also be accessible to American ships—a recognition of parity in foreign commerce. Even more consequential was the acknowledgment of extraterritoriality for American citizens, granting them immunity from Japanese law and placing them solely under the jurisdiction of the Consul-General for any offenses committed on Japanese soil.

These concessions, however, were won against a backdrop of intense pressure on Japan's State Council of Five, the Shogunate's highest advisory body. In the 1850s, this council—composed of the senior daimyōs and officials entrusted with governing the country in the Shogun's name—was responsible for implementing policy while safeguarding Japan's centuries-old isolationist traditions.

They faced an almost impossible balance: adhere strictly to Tokugawa orthodoxy or concede to foreign demands and risk national humiliation. In this culture of absolute accountability, failure could carry the ultimate penalty. Should the Shogun reject a council proposal twice, the responsible members were expected to commit hara-kiri, or ritual suicide, as a demonstration of loyalty, honor, and personal responsibility. Hara-kiri involved disembowelment with a short sword, often performed in a formal, highly codified ceremony—a grim testament to the gravity of political failure in Tokugawa Japan.

Henry observed with keen interest how these small but significant concessions were forcing the rigid Council of Five to bend to the emerging norms of international diplomacy. In navigating this high-stakes environment, the American legation had not merely secured trade advantages; they were subtly reshaping the power dynamics of the Shogunate itself. Each agreement, each acknowledgment of foreign law and parity, chipped away at centuries of isolation, signaling the slow but undeniable transformation of Japan's political and cultural order.

When the American clipper *Messenger Bird* anchored in March, it became the first ship to take advantage of the new six percent exchange rate. The Japanese, however, expected the price of American goods to fall by two-thirds, failing to grasp the simple principle that American goods were already priced according to the just value of the dollar.

But the wall had cracks. Henry could now walk the streets, enter houses, and speak with the common people without opposition. The young girls, formerly so shy, no longer fled. The beasts of burden, formerly so fearful of the foreigner, could no longer distinguish him from their own masters. Only the dogs, Henry noted wryly, remained fiercely faithful to their anti-foreign principles.

The Consul-General had won the War of Politeness. Now, they could turn their full attention to the ultimate prize: Edo.

9

The Right to Ride

The long months of monastic siege, surveillance, and polite warfare had finally given way to purpose. Henry had endured the silence and the heat, and in May 1857, he found himself a man transformed—no longer the penniless man, but a figure whose presence, in the rigid social calculus of Japan, commanded cautious respect.

The most tangible symbol of his new station in Japan arrived not through a diplomatic courier but by way of a four-legged beast. On May 21, 1857, Henry wrote, "Today I find myself the happy owner of a horse—a thoroughbred!" he scribbled in his journal, the humor barely masking his immense satisfaction. The cost was $27.41, a sum he translated into the enormous boast of 128,000 kash, Chinese coins.

Henry, standing tall, broad-shouldered, and fair-haired, now found himself astride a fine animal, a privilege in Japan reserved only for samurai and nobles. In a country where every square inch of space and every social rank was meticulously defined, the horse was a declaration: Lord Heusken, the Dutchman turned American, had arrived.

His transformation was complete. The black clothes shining with old age, the cherished shoes with perfect ventilation—those relics of his impoverished New York days—were gone. Now, he was followed not by hostile police, but by the watchful eyes of villagers, many of whom could not suppress their hidden amusement at the tall foreigner's less-than-masterful horsemanship. Yet, he rode anyway. The laughter did not matter; the right to ride, the symbolic ascent into the hierarchy of this feudal world, was itself a major, personal victory.

"If I go on this way," he mused, savoring the incredible, intoxicating taste of his elevated standing, "why shouldn't I maintain my own carriage and ask in marriage the Emperor's only daughter?"

It is crucial to understand that Henry's newfound air of grandeur and privilege was rigidly backed up by the customs of Japanese society itself. At this time in ancient Japan, horses were powerful symbols of prestige, and the act of riding them was an exclusive privilege reserved for the highest-ranking members of society, specifically the aristocracy and the samurai warrior class.

Only these elites possessed the necessary access to the resources needed to breed, train, and maintain the elaborate equestrian equipment. Commoners and women rarely, if ever, rode horses in a formal capacity, and saddle riding was specifically forbidden for non-samurai. This restriction served a powerful societal function, reinforcing the rigid social divisions within Japanese society. Therefore, every time Henry rode his horse, he was visibly claiming a status that placed him above nearly all common Japanese citizens. This profound statement was not lost on the highly observant populace.

The Diplomatic Sacrifice

This personal triumph coincided with the immense, hard-won victory of their mission. For ten long months, Harris had played the game of silence and endurance, refusing to be budged by the innumerable delays and heated arguments of the Governors.

On June 17, 1857, after ten long months of patience, persistence, and endless negotiation, the Consul-General had finally forced the Governors of Shimoda to put pen to paper. The arguments had been heated; the delays, endless. The Japanese bureaucracy, as always, had invented obstacle after obstacle. In the fray, the Governor, Bingo no Kami, had lost his position, recalled in disgrace, and replaced by Nakamura, Dewa no Kami. The former governor had been reassigned to Edo as Governor of Reparations—a quiet exile, Henry noted wryly, for a man caught in the diplomatic crossfire.

The treaty, slim yet monumental, carried weight far beyond its pages. The first article opened the port of Nagasaki to American ships, allowing them to procure food and coal and make repairs—critical provisions for the steaming iron leviathans that now plied the Pacific. The second article granted permanent residence in Shimoda and Hakodate for American citizens, with the right to station a Vice Consul in the latter. Henry's mind leapt ahead: the first American missionaries would soon follow the merchants, for they too would arrive as citizens, indistinguishable under the law from ship captains or traders.

The third article corrected the currency imbalance that had long vexed American merchants: gold for gold, silver for silver, with six percent added for coinage. This victory reduced the inflated cost of the ichibu to less than thirty-five cents on the dollar. The fourth article granted extraterritoriality, allowing

Americans to be judged solely by their Consul. The fifth author-ized the use of merchandise in lieu of currency at Shimoda, Hakodate, and Nagasaki, ensuring ships could trade even when coffers were empty.

The sixth article confirmed that the Consul-General could travel beyond the strict seven ri limits of Shimoda Bay, though he was expected to honor any requests for temporary delays. Note that a "ri" is a traditional unit of distance, officially stand-ardized to about 3.93 kilometers or 2.44 miles. Henry read this as more than a practical allowance; it was a symbolic crack in Japan's centuries-old isolation. The Treaty of Kanagawa effec-tively created a sphere of freedom around Shimoda, centered on Center Island, from which the Consul-General could eventu-ally penetrate into the interior—Edo, Miyako, and beyond.

Finally, the seventh article allowed the Consul-General and his household to purchase directly from merchants, bypassing the labyrinthine channels of Japanese intermediaries. Should Edo eventually extend this right to all Americans, it would be nothing less than the foundation of a true Treaty of Commerce with Japan. Henry could almost see it: the Consul-General, armed with full authority to negotiate, would soon step forward to formally present credentials and begin talks that would for-ever reshape the relationship between the United States and the Empire of Japan.

It was a triumph, quietly revolutionary in its effect—a victory not won with cannon or warships, but with patience, strategy, and the relentless application of diplomacy.

Although this treaty was secured, their work was far from complete; it served merely as a stepping stone toward the true objective of a formal commercial treaty that would finally and fully open Japan to the world. They were not content with a few minor articles negotiated outside the capital, which the Japanese hoped would placate the Americans into believing their mission was finished. Both Harris and Heusken understood that while this was a step in the right direction, their ultimate goal remained a grand agreement signed in Edo with the Shogun himself, ensuring Japan was once and for all integrated into the global community.

It was also in June that Henry and Harris discovered they were no longer the only Americans residing in Japan. On June 23, 1857, they received a letter from E. E. Rice, who informed them that he had been appointed the U.S. commercial agent at Hakodate, the other port open to American trade. Rice wrote that he had "hoisted his flag" there and intended to assist American vessels stopping for provisions and coal, most of which were U.S. whaling ships at the time.

This correspondence was noteworthy for another reason: it was the first letter Harris had received from an American in ten months. Though it was a relief to know that another countryman now lived on Japanese shores, both Harris and Henry longed for letters from home rather than from another foreigner enduring the same isolation. Still, Rice's arrival was a welcome development. His mission, however, focused on helping U.S. ships secure supplies—while Harris and Henry carried the heavier burden of diplomacy and of opening Japan to the world.

The Final Maneuver

But the victory was incomplete. The ultimate goal—Edo— remained locked behind the Shogun's authority.

Article Six of the new Convention addressed this crucial point. The Japanese Government recognized the right of the

Consul-General to pass beyond the seven ri limits (16 English miles). However, at their request, Harris consented to a delay in exercising that right. This was a critical distinction: the right was conceded; only the timing was negotiable.

Harris knew the delay could not be long. The occasion came on July 9, 1857.

Harris had demanded a satisfactory answer regarding the letter of the President of the United States to the Shogun, which he was the official bearer of. The Governors replied that they were empowered to receive that letter and that one of them would deliver it in person to Edo.

Then, fate handed Harris a brilliant diplomatic weapon. A few days earlier, the Council of State had sent a letter to Harris, and the Governors—citing the rigid demands of Japanese etiquette—refused to hand it to Henry, demanding that it be delivered only to the person to whom it was addressed. Harris had been forced to wait for his health to recover before receiving it.

Harris seized the contradiction, his words striking like cold steel through the fabric of their etiquette.

"What!" he thundered, staring down the Governors in his antechamber. "You yourselves refuse to hand my secretary a letter signed by the legislative authority of this Empire, and you demand that it be delivered only to the person to whom it is addressed? While I, the bearer of a letter signed by the Chief Executive of a powerful nation, am refused permission to hand it to the person to whom it is addressed?"

The logic was flawless, devastating. The Governors were trapped by their own protocol. Henry, translating the blistering logic, saw their faces flush with shame and confusion. Their own customs had undone them.

Harris delivered his final ultimatum: "I demand that I may deliver the letter from the President to His Majesty, the Emperor of Japan, in person, and I can give it to no one else."

The Governors were powerless. Their much-vaunted "full powers" did not cover such an unprecedented act. Shinano no Kami—the remaining Governor—was forced to immediately leave for Edo to consult the Great Council of State.

The long siege was over. The breakthrough had been achieved not by cannon or coin, but by principle and linguistic maneuver. The way to Edo was not yet open, but the decision had been wrenched from Shimoda and placed squarely before the highest authorities in the Shogunate.

10

The Shogun's Reply

The summer of 1857 was a period of exquisite, sustained torture for Henry. Harris and Henry had played their cards—Harris's ultimatum, the Convention of Shimoda, the unanswerable logic that demanded the letter be delivered to the Shogun in person—and now they were forced to endure the agonizing stillness of the Japanese reply.

The American consulate was a hollow, echoing shell. Though they heard of another American, Mr. Rice, in Hakodate, the news only deepened their profound isolation. Henry desperately longed for a ship, a tangible link to the outside world, and most of all, a letter from his mother, the distant echo of family that kept his heart tethered across the ocean.

On July 10, 1857, a cannon shot from atop the lookout mountain shattered the stillness.

Henry leaped from his chair, adrenaline overwhelming months of heat and boredom. After two years without a word, he imagined an immense packet, seeing his mother's handwriting, hearing from his friends. He ran, singing and climbing at a gallop up the neighboring mountain, his eyes fixed on the unlimited vantage point. There, penetrating the fog, he discovered the triple masts of a large ship.

He returned to the Consul, breathless and triumphant, only for the ship to disappear, having changed its course toward the northeast. The next day, Henry resumed his futile search. No ship, no letters, no tidings. He returned to the temple, embarrassed and confused, swearing—a little too late—that he would never again allow hope to betray him so cruelly.

The Comedy of Misery

Amidst the high-stakes diplomacy, Henry found himself mired in the low comedy of his new status. His thoroughbred horse, the glorious symbol of his ascent, became an immediate source of frustration. He had rented a stable for an enormous sum of four hundred *seni*, but his improvised cotton saddle, made to avoid the uncomfortable Japanese type, kept sliding under the horse's belly.

His first rides were agony. The roads were abominable—strewn with stones, holes, and steep grades, making anything faster than a slow pace impossible. After a second ride, Henry discovered the Japanese groom had used only one rope to tie the saddle, which had cut into the horse's back in a frightful manner. It would be lame for months.

Harris, with paternal kindness, loaned Henry his own steed, only for that horse to immediately wrench its shoulder, slipping on a steep grade. "He will be lame for the rest of his days," the Japanese veterinary surgeon declared.

The Final, Grinding Battle

On August 25, 1857, the wait ended. Shinano no Kami arrived from Edo.

The meeting two days later was the climax of the long, cold war of words. The Governor began with a grand concession: the High Council had finally agreed to receive the Consul-General in Edo. But the victory was immediately qualified: Harris could not hand the letter to the Shogun himself; the High Council would accept it on his behalf.

Harris refused, but the Governors argued that the Shogun never personally met with foreigners, additionally, the eighteen princes of Japan were opposed, and that granting the demand would create disturbances in the Empire. They urged Harris to send a letter explaining all of this to the Secretary of State in Washington, and then to wait to hear back from him before they decided on how to move forward. This was a clear attempt to delay and shift responsibility, knowing this would take months or years.

Harris rejected the proposal, citing historical precedents, noting that Father Valignani, bearer of a letter from the Viceroy of Goa, had been received by the Shogun. The Governors simply denied that the archives contained any such record. The frustration was immense. The officials, fearing ruin, reiterated their request for Harris to disclose the critical matters he was bearing to them, arguing that Shinano no Kami had guaranteed to the Great Council that the Consul would tell them the U.S. demands instead of telling the Shogun directly.

Harris turned to Henry. "Did I ever promise to communicate my business before receiving in writing permission to go to Edo and deliver the letter into the Shogun's hands?"

Henry knew his precise role was to be the memory of the Legation, the linguistic anchor against their planned amnesia.

Thus, Henry confirmed that Harris had always demanded to go to Edo and give his demands directly to the Shogun. Henry's words striking the Governors like physical blows. Then Harris stressed, "Why answer, 'You cannot deliver the letter into the hands of the Shogun,' if I have never requested it?"

The Governors had no reply and retreated into evasions, their shame turning to desperate pleading. They warned him that their inability to transmit a satisfactory answer might lead to them being forced to commit *hara-kiri*—to cut open their own stomachs and die. Henry, once again, realized the lethal cost of this diplomatic game.

The Unshakable Ultimatum

Harris, ever perceptive to the subtle levers of fear and manipulation, refused to yield. On August 31, 1857, he laid out two options with deliberate precision: he could either communicate the essential matters before traveling to Edo while still delivering the letter to the Shogun personally, or he could proceed immediately to Edo, present the letter to the Prime Minister in the Shogun's presence, and address the Shogun directly, allowing His Majesty to respond in turn.

The Governors pleaded with him not demand a meeting with the Shogun. Angered by their attempts at coercion, Harris declared that threats held no sway over him and that he would remain true to the honor he owed his country. Two days later, on September 2, 1857, Harris—the master tactician—rescinded both options in a carefully worded letter.

He expressed dissatisfaction with his own prior concessions and made it clear that he had no further proposals: it was now up to the Governors to make their move. By doing so, he turned their obstinacy against them, using their refusal to accept his conditions as leverage. Defeated and desperate, the Governors sent Moriyama, the chief interpreter, to plead for reconsideration. But Harris, unflinching, had Henry deliver the final, sealed letter, asserting his authority and leaving the Japanese officials with no choice but to comply.

The Triumph of the Sea

The diplomatic standoff was broken on September 7, 1857. The Governors agreed to send a messenger to Edo, asking the government for permission to make Harris the following proposal: He will go to Edo and deliver the letter personally to the Premier in the presence of the Shogun. The long fight had yielded Harris's second proposal, the essential breach of etiquette that paved the way to the capital.

The victory was instantly sealed by providence. A cannon shot rang out from the lookout mountain. This time, Henry would not be denied.

Clambering up the mountain in his slippers beneath a burning sun, he confirmed the report: a large vessel was indeed making for the port. However, the origin of the Western sailing ship remained uncertain. Fearing that a rival mission might be arriving to seize the glory intended for the United States, he determined that he must head out immediately to identify the interloper.

At twilight, he took a boat and ten oarsmen, rowing out into the open sea. Hours later, guided only by moonlight and the promise of civilization, Henry heard a sound that made his heart leap: the familiar tune of "Yankee Doodle."

He was aboard the American corvette USS *Portsmouth*, greeted by Captain Foote and the officers. Henry spent two hours in a glorious torrent of conversation learning about what was going on in the world. By the end of those hours he was no longer the "poor ignoramus" who knew nothing world events. Finally, at two in the morning, he returned to the consulate, carrying a massive package of letters and newspapers.

The mail, delayed for a year, brought the ultimate relief: "Two letters from my mother, Praise God! She is happy and fully recovered; she is alive."

The *Portsmouth* remained for a fleeting four days—a glorious interlude of formal dinners and official business that proved to be an exceptionally frantic period. Even as Captain Foote regaled them with vivid accounts of his daring capture of the Chinese Barrier Forts, both Harris and Henry were overwhelmed by the task of drafting official responses and preparing dispatches for the Department of State that would be sent back with the ship. Henry noted that he was entirely unable to attend to his private letters; however, he did find the opportunity to ask Captain Foote to use his influence with the U.S. government to help secure the back pay owed to him since his departure from New York. It appeared that throughout much of the long and arduous voyage to Japan, Henry had received little to no salary. Now, established as a gentleman in Japan—with a horse at his disposal and the requisite trappings of his new station—he finally sought the compensation due for those months of service.

On September 12, 1857, the *Portsmouth* departed, leaving behind a profound sense of renewal and energy. The Shogun's doors were now open, Henry had heard from his mother, the sea was no longer silent, and Henry Heusken, the U.S. Diplomat, was finally free to ride the road to Edo with Harris. The next act of the epic was about to begin.

II

The Triumph and the Tonsure

The waiting was over. On September 23, 1857, the Governors of Shimoda surrendered.

In the final meeting at the *Goyosho*, the message from Edo arrived, conceding everything Harris had demanded: "We will be received in Edo with the greatest honors." Harris, the relentless man of principle, would be granted an audience with the Taikun—the title meaning "great lord," a diplomatic nod to the Shogun's sovereign authority. He would deliver a speech, and Henry, the essential linguist, would perform the final, crowning act of their two-year struggle: handing the letter of the President to the Japanese President of the Great Council, Hotta, Bitchū no Kami.

Yet, even in triumph, the Shogunate attempted one final, desperate assertion of its supremacy. There was a fruitless attempt to make the Consul pay his respects in the Japanese manner: on his knees with his head bent low.

Harris, his composure a suit of iron, positively refused. He would pay the same homage to the Taikun of Japan as was presented by an Ambassador to the most powerful monarchs of the

West, but nothing more. The line was drawn; the dignity of the American republic would not be sacrificed to Asiatic custom. It was a victory of honor, ensuring that when they finally entered the capital, it would be as equals, not as supplicants.

The stage was set. The date for their departure was fixed as Monday, November 23.

The Cartography of Humiliation

The ensuing month of preparations was a dizzying descent into the minutiae of Japanese protocol. Shinano no Kami and Moriyama, the chief interpreter, returned from Edo with a multitude of arrangements, most of which were exceedingly childish.

Japanese diplomacy, Henry observed, treated the momentous journey like an exercise in cartography and choreography. They provided two meticulous maps of the Imperial Palace, charting every step of their triumphal route through the inner sanctum.

The ritual of the norimon (palanquin) was a prime example of their obsessive focus on rank. The Shogunate defined the exact yards where each person of importance must leave his norimon and walk—a public demonstration of subservience to the capital.

Henry, as Harris's secretary, would leave his norimon at the outer enclosure. Harris, as the Plenipotentiary, would leave his at the inner wall, a spot shared only with the Governor of Shimoda and the Prince of Shinano. The rule was inviolable: everyone—even the highest Princes of the Blood—must walk from the inner wall to the Palace entrance, save only for the three brothers of the King (Shogun) who were permitted to disembark "a little further on."

The irony was not lost on Henry: they were fighting to open a nation, yet they were consumed by a ceremonial dance dictating the precise location where they must plant their feet.

The only concession to hygiene came at the top of the stairway. They would remove their soiled foreign shoes and replace them with brand new ones before stepping onto the sacred matting—the *tatami* that served the Japanese as table, bed, and floor. Henry could not object, noting wryly that they were fortunate the Japanese did not insist they go shoeless entirely.

And in a final act of control, the speech of the Ambassador and the reply of the Taikun were to be agreed in advance. The momentous, historic exchange would be a controlled script, designed to eliminate surprise. Even the translation would be direct: Harris would speak in English, and the monarch would reply in Japanese, without the dreaded intermediation of an interpreter. Henry, the very hinge of the mission, was to be reduced to a silent sentinel, ensuring the integrity of the ceremonial exchange.

The Fall and The Tonsure

Amidst this feverish, detailed planning, Henry's quest nearly ended in a disaster of accidental self-mutilation.

His continued attempts to master his horse on the miserable roads of Japan proved treacherous. "Yesterday I nearly killed myself," he recorded. His steed stumbled, fell, and Henry was projected over its head to the ground, making a complete somersault. He landed headfirst on the rocks strewn across the road.

He scrambled back onto the horse, blood dripping from his head to the astonishment of the villagers of Kakizaki. The sharp stone had made a rather deep cut precisely at the spot where the Catholic clergy wear the tonsure.

The accident was a moment of profound personal risk. Still, Henry's immediate fear was diplomatic, not physical: "They are going to mistake you for a Jesuit or a Franciscan in disguise," he thought, knowing the deep, historical Japanese antipathy to the banned Christian faith. A missionary, even in disguise, would be locked up in a cage for life, and his diplomatic character instantly revoked. The cut was a permanent scar, a mark of the thin, bloody line separating the diplomat from the condemned religious intruder.

The Final Uniformity

In the days leading up to the departure, Henry observed the unnerving uniformity of the Japanese life they were about to infiltrate. Their culture seemed to be governed entirely by decree: "They take their breakfast, lunch, and dinner all exactly at the same hour. They change clothes four times a year on the same day."

Even natural phenomena seemed regulated: "Apparently they go even further, for today everybody without exception has a cold, certainly by order of the government."

This absolute societal control, this disciplined submission to arbitrary order, was the formidable force Harris and Henry were about to challenge. They were two men carrying a letter, a few principles, and the audacious belief in free commerce and human rights, marching into the heart of a civilization built upon unyielding, absolute law.

The long, agonizing siege of Shimoda was over. The Temple was abandoned. On November 23, they would leave the confines of the peninsula, their procession a narrow, bold line of color and purpose slicing into the monochrome tapestry of feudal Japan. The grand, historic march to Edo, the capital of two million souls, was about to begin.

12

The Luminous Serpent

The day of liberation and reckoning arrived on November 23, 1857.

Long before the sun cleared the mountains, the compound of Gyokusenji Temple—their long-suffering prison—filled with a throng of people: litter-bearers, soldiers, coolies. It was a mobilization of feudal Japan dedicated solely to conveying two foreigners to the highest seat of power. Kikuna Sennojo, an Imperial officer of the second class, presented himself to Harris, whom they now respectfully styled "the Ambassador," and declared himself ready to lead the party to Edo.

Henry, having entrusted their meager household goods to their four Chinese servants, stepped out to join the procession. It was an arrangement of meticulous, hierarchical order:

First, the Imperial Authority: Kikuna, followed by his soldier bearing the pike.

Second, the American Embassy: Townsend Harris on horseback, preceded by a standard-bearer carrying the Stars and Stripes, and followed by two samurai, an armed umbrella-bearer, and a shoe-bearer.

Third, the U.S. Diplomat: Henry Heusken on his recently acquired steed, followed by his own retinue of two samurai, his valet, and his umbrella-bearer.

Finally, the Japanese officers and the norimon of Vice-Governor Wakana Myosaburo terminated the single-file line—a small, potent wedge of Western principle slicing into the vastness of the Tokugawa domain.

They left the quiet valleys of Shimoda, skirting the river and admiring the rich crop of rice—the great, shimmering fields that had just been cut, the lifeblood of the Empire destined to fill the Imperial warehouses. After resting at a *miya* (Shinto temple) and dispensing the obligatory tips to officials in accordance with the ancient Japanese custom, they pressed deeper into the Idzu Peninsula.

The Ordeal of the Mountain

The journey was immediately revealed to be an ordeal of granite and mud.

The next day, they set out to ascend Mount Amagi, a colossal barrier of five thousand feet. They climbed steep paths above deep chasms, the route carved into the rock like a genuine staircase. Henry finally understood the strategic brilliance of the Shogunate: by choosing Shimoda, they had given the Americans a port inaccessible by land to the rest of Japan. The mountains, placed by nature between the town and the rest of Japan, made extensive land travel impossible.

Henry dismounted, preferring to walk, realizing that his grandeur has its disadvantages. His elaborate retinue—the two samurai, the shoe-bearer, the umbrella-bearer—still followed him like his own shadow, their presence a perpetual, stifling burden.

"What wouldn't I give to be an ordinary traveler," he groaned inwardly, "and go through these mountains leisurely, stopping at attractive spots, or stretching myself out on the grass according to my fancy?"

But if he stopped, the entire procession had to stop. The fear of having his entourage step on his heels, or of making an intimate relationship between my nose and the mud of the road, was a constant, low-grade torture. He recalled the wisdom of the fictional squire in Don Quixote: Sancho Panza was right when he resigned his governorship.

The Mountain of Mountains

As they descended the mountain, emerging from the clouds that perpetually hovered over the summit, the countryside unfolded below in ravishing valleys. Then, rounding a mountain, Henry caught a glimpse through the foliage of a few pine trees: a white peak that gleamed in the sun. Fujiyama.

Henry stopped his horse, carried away by an outburst of unbridled American enthusiasm. He tore off his hat and cried: "Great, glorious Fujiyama! Glory forever to the mountain of mountains of the Pacific Sea!"

He found himself instantly placing the mountain in the global ledger of majesty. There were peaks three times higher than Fuji, and the glaciers of the Himalayas were magnificent, but they were hidden in inaccessible desolation. But here, Fuji rose from a smiling countryside covered with abundant crops and ancient groves of giant camphor trees. Its pure outline, two perfect, symmetrical lines towards the sky, stood above all rivals.

Amagi, which they had just crossed after a most challenging day, seemed only a small hill, hardly worth mentioning.

Henry, the romantic diplomat, felt the mountain capturing his soul, a symbol of the profound, untouched beauty of this nation he was charged with changing.

The Moral Cost of Honor

The brief, exhilarating moment of freedom was crushed the next day. Finding a level road near Yugashima, Henry and Harris, impatient with the funereal pace of the ceremony, spurred their mounts, leaving samurai, norimons, Vice-Governors, and all emblems of decorum behind them. The spectacle shocked the poor Japanese, who could not comprehend why men of such high stations would let themselves be carried away by speedy horses like poor plebeians.

But freedom came at a heavy moral price. From Mishima onwards, they traveled the famous Tōkaidō, the Great Highway of Japan, now miraculously repaired and absolutely deserted by command of the government. Before each village, authorities lined up, bowing their foreheads to the ground. Policemen, armed with iron rods, constantly cleared the way.

As they rode, heralds walking ahead continually shouted the humiliating command: *"Shita ni iro, shita ni iro!"* Kneel down, kneel down!

Henry traveled for seven days amidst a kneeling population. The common people—men, women, and children—knelt and remained in an attitude of deepest respect until they had passed. He saw white-haired old men bending their knees and young girls turning their lovely faces towards the ground.

The sight began to disgust him.

"It is certainly an excessive honor to see all the beauties of Japan on their knees before oneself," he wrote, filled with revulsion. He saw the full, terrifying power of the government, which could command all the people to bow down before two foreigners, simply to underscore its own authority. Henry, the advocate of freedom and equality, yearned to join them: "If I had been allowed at least to kneel with her, this thing would have had a different complexion."

The Final Challenge

The last significant obstacle before the Kanto Plain was the Hakone Barrier, an ancient station where Imperial officers searched travelers to and from the capital. The most powerful princes, even the Prince of Satsuma, submitted to this inspection.

The officials informed Harris that they would open his norimon door to glance inside. Harris, citing his extraterritoriality and his status as the President's representative, refused to submit to such treatment. He demanded to pass through the barrier with his norimon door unopened, or he would not pass at all.

After a tense, two-hour standoff, the officers conceded Harris's right of inviolability. However, the Japanese, ever masters of protocol, reserved the right to open Henry's norimon.

The honor was granted, yet the victory was immediately sabotaged. As they passed the gate, Harris's personal valet, Takizo—unaware of the high diplomatic struggle—opened the Ambassador's norimon door and closed it immediately, believing he was subject to the custom like everyone else. Harris was furious, believing the Japanese had broken their word, but it was merely a failure of cultural translation—a valet's fearful obedience to the ancient law of the land.

Delayed until nine o'clock at night, the procession became a marvelous, chaotic sight: a luminous serpent winding down the mountain, torches and lanterns lighting their way toward Odawara. Policemen pounded their iron rods, honoring the American diplomatic delegation before them.

They had won the fight to be received, endured the mountains, and survived the moral horror of the kneeling people. Now, they were on the Tōkaidō, the great, smooth highway, where they saw Japanese-built corvettes—old-fashioned models that testified to a slow, deliberate modernization. Ahead lay the plain, and beyond it, the vast, mysterious complexity of Edo. The final conversation—the one that would truly shape history— was imminent.

13

The Norimon of Japhet

The journey from the relative comfort of the Mannenya at Kawasaki to the gates of Edo on the morning of Monday, November 30, 1857, was the final, inevitable approach to the heart of the closed world.

Edo, the seat of the Tokugawa Shogunate, was a phenomenon of the age—a sprawling metropolis of over a million inhabitants, a labyrinth of wooden buildings, narrow alleys, and the immense, silent power of the Edo Castle. It was a city where tradition and order were not merely respected, but ruthlessly enforced. Samurai in their distinct dress patrolled, and the urban landscape, though pulsing with life, was designed to protect Japan from outside influence, preserving centuries of isolation under the *sakoku* policy.

Harris, despite Henry's preference for riding, had judged that their entry must be made by norimon—the palanquin—as more suitable to their diplomatic rank. This proved Henry's final physical torment, as he suffered all kinds of tortures, not knowing what to do with his legs inside the short, tight litter.

The Million Silent Witnesses

After crossing the Logo River by boat and passing the silent, austere execution ground near Shinagawa—cleared, Henry suspected, by government order—they began the seven-mile journey through the city's outskirts.

The procession was now a formal entity of immense symbolic weight, headed by the Vice-Governor in his norimon, followed by Harris, surrounded by ten samurai, preceded by the flag of the United States, and carried by twelve alternating men. Then came Henry in his agonizing norimon, surrounded by his three guards, his valet, and his shoe-bearer.

The throng of people that bordered the highway from Shinagawa was continuous, pressing in on both sides. Henry, risking a glance from the confines of his box, estimated the assembled multitude at a million.

Despite this immense number, not a voice was heard. A respectful, awestruck silence reigned over all. They stooped down, one over the other, in order to glance into the norimons of the foreign devils.

The city's security measures, designed to control the emotional outbursts of two million people, were brilliantly simple. The streets of Edo were divided into sections, each sealed by a barrier. As the procession passed through, the barrier was closed behind them, ensuring they were always within a sort of tiny fortress, preventing too many people from gathering at one spot. Local police, clad in dark blue blouses featuring harlequin figures, accompanied them, pounding the street with iron rods that served as both an honor guard and a warning.

Henry was swept with profound admiration for the sheer order that reigned over this vast multitude. If people pressed too far, an officer shaking his paper fan sufficed to cause hundreds of people to step back. There were no crushing crowds, no profanity, no thrown stones—a chilling contrast to the expected chaos of any great Western capital in the same situation.

The Contradiction of the Crowd

The faces Henry glimpsed—men, women, boys, and young girls—showed no signs of antipathy or anger, but a pure, acute curiosity. He was convinced that the isolation of Japan was not due to the people's hatred of the foreigner, but to the profound veneration they held for ancient, obsolete laws and the obstinacy of old-school princes.

As his norimon was carried through this sea of humanity, Henry felt the full, strange weight of his new existence. His thoughts took him back to his childhood, when he would brave the cold and jostling crowds just to catch a glimpse of the distant carriage of a King for a few seconds.

"Ah, I was once envious of even stable boys," he reflected, the absurdity washing over him. "And today here I am in the position of the aforementioned personages. An entire people are shoving and jostling each other, leaving their daily occupations, dying of hunger and fatigue. And for what? In order to be able to glance into two norimons containing two children of Japhet."

He noted the final proof of the Shogunate's iron control over its nobles: when passing the fashionable district and the palaces of the *Daimyos*, he was not allowed to see the noble girls. The blinds and bars were drawn tight, only allowing the vague outlines of a throng of heads to be seen, save for a few rare exceptions when a charitable blind revealed a pair of black eyes, or a small hand as white as the snows of Fujiyama.

The Theatrical Rehearsal

At four in the afternoon, the procession halted at the gate of their hotel, situated within the third enclosure of the Imperial Castle. This was the very inner sanctum of the Shogun's power.

Harris was immediately welcomed by Shinano no Kami, who yielded to fatigue and accepted the prepared letter announcing the Ambassador's arrival and requesting an audience with the Shogun.

They were shown to their quarters—a deliberate concession to Western discomfort. Though the rooms followed the Japanese austere style of matting and paper, they had been outfitted with chairs, tables, and bedframes, things utterly unknown in Japan, built expressly for them.

However, the work was not over. In spite of the fatigue, Shinano no Kami insisted they immediately proceed with a full, bizarre rehearsal of the reception for the Ambassador Extraordinary—the final test before the grand audience.

Henry and Harris were led through a regular theatrical rehearsal. They practiced the exact number of bows in the vestibule, the proper movement forward, and the precise spot where Mr. Harris was to stand. The entire ceremony was a quadrille of courtesy, a hyper-specific choreographing of rank and dignity.

The Japanese Ambassador Extraordinary—whom Henry deemed an extraordinary man indeed—would stand at a particular spot to speak *in the name of the Taikun*, and then immediately change places when he spoke *in his own name*. Harris was begged to abide by the same formalities, changing places as the others did. Henry, utterly confused by the hyper-ritualized absurdity, had only vague ideas about the whole matter, save that they were to bow, move, and change places.

Bonbons and the Brink of History

The final, fatiguing ordeal took place the next day, December 1, 1857, with the actual reception of the Ambassador Extraordinary. Harris received him, kneeling officials forming a human pyramid of subservience below him. The Ambassador, after the endless bows and shifts of position, finally delivered the gift from His Majesty the Taikun.

Harris hastily opened the box, the reward for two years of loneliness, struggle, and iron-willed diplomacy. The box, Henry noted with cynical amusement, contained a great quantity of bonbons—candy. There was enough to fill a confectioner's shop and make ill an infinite number of children.

The gift was an act of childish simplicity, the absurdity of which was overwhelming given the gravity of the occasion. Yet, the exhausted diplomats consumed the bonbons on the eve of their historic audience. The theatre was complete, the rules had been learned, and the final night was spent resting within the ancient walls of the Shogun's palace, preparing for the moment that would change the course of history for both Japan and the world.

14

The Salon of Forty-Five Mats

The great diplomatic engine of the Shogunate ground into motion. Having been received with the appropriate ceremonial drama, Harris and Henry were now immersed in the bureaucratic heart of Edo.

Eight Commissioners had been appointed, an inner circle of high-ranking officials charged with containing the unpredictable force of the American Ambassador and ensuring all business passed through their meticulous hands. Among them were influential men—Hayashi, Daigaku no Kami; Hizen no Kami; and Shinano no Kami—all reporting to their chief, Toki, Tamba no Kami.

On Wednesday, December 2, 1857, the Minister of Foreign Affairs provided the final, concrete detail: The audience will take place on the seventh of this month at nine o'clock in the morning. The date was set. The long, frustrating diplomatic war, waged with norimon rides and tea ceremonies, would be settled in less than a week.

Harris, with his customary blend of politeness and strategic aggression, immediately secured a pre-audience meeting. On

December 3, he advised the Minister of his desire to pay him a visit and, crucially, sent a copy of the President's letter to the Emperor within the same envelope. This was a necessary courtesy, ensuring the Japanese were prepared for the momentous contents, but also a strategic move that preempted any last-minute challenge regarding the letter's nature.

The Minister's Threshold

The actual meeting on Friday, December 4, 1857, was the moment Henry and Harris crossed the highest threshold of Japanese political power they had yet encountered. Their norimons moved along the massive walls of the Castle, past wide streets lined by the palaces of the Princes, which looked like huge barracks, until they reached the residence of the Minister.

Entering the palace of Hotta, Prince of Bitchū, Henry was struck by the seamless hierarchy. A great number of officers were seated in order on the mats by the entrance, and as the two Americans passed, this multitude of heads bent to the ground, as if at a given signal. It was the prostration Henry had seen in Siam, but executed with Japanese efficiency and silent, absolute discipline.

After exchanging bows with the eight Commissioners in a suite of rooms, they were led to the true arena: a vast chamber called the Salon of Forty-Five Mats.

The Prince of Bitchū himself was standing near the door. After a formal exchange of bows, he guided Harris to the other end of the salon. The seating arrangement was the most significant diplomatic victory Harris had yet won: the Prince sat on a small taboret on one side, and Harris and Henry sat on two chairs on the other.

In this room, where every gesture was usually governed by the distance from the floor, the American Ambassador sat at eye-level with the highest minister in the Shogunate—a concession that acknowledged the sovereignty of the United States.

The War of Smiles

The Minister, Hotta, Prince of Bitchū, was a man of most charming manners, with a gentle countenance and a disarming smile, though Henry noted that he stammered a little and seemed inwardly quite ill at ease. The source of his discomfort was clear: he, who was accustomed to seeing everyone prostrate at his feet, was receiving foreigners who were occupying seats of the same level as his own.

The ensuing conversation was a dizzying dance of interpretation. Moriyama Takichiro, the chief interpreter, knelt beside the former Governor, Shinano no Kami. Every word Harris spoke was first translated by Henry from English into Dutch, then repeated by Moriyama to Shinano no Kami, and finally by the Prince to the Minister. It was an inefficient, frustrating mechanism of caution, designed to give the Japanese bureaucracy three layers of protection and denial.

Harris used this moment to present his demands in full. He handed them a paper containing the speech he proposed to deliver at the audience with the Shogun. The Minister and his retinue retired to deliberate, leaving Harris and Henry alone.

Upon their return, the Minister presented Harris with a paper through the intermediary of Shinano no Kami—the prepared answer which the Taikun would make to Mr. Harris's speech on the day of the audience. The entire historic moment was to be a choreographed exchange, ensuring the Shogun uttered nothing unpredictable.

Hotta and Harris engaged in further, polite conversation, but Henry, watching the Minister's gentle face and observing the careful, measured movements of the twelve servants who entered carrying objects aloft, understood the enormous political risk Hotta was undertaking. The Minister was the man willing to break with centuries of tradition to speak with the world.

The St. Nicholas Consolation

On Sunday, December 6, 1857, a messenger arrived at the American legation, which is what Henry was now calling their rooms in the palace, carrying a letter from Mr. Donker Curtius, the Dutch Commissioner. Inside was a smaller, far more precious envelope—one addressed to Henry, written in the familiar hand of his mother. The effect was overwhelming. After a year of near-total isolation in this strange and distant land, hemmed in by formality and suspicion, the sight of that tender, looping script pierced through the cold reserve that duty had built around him. It was, as Henry later wrote, "a good St. Nicholas after all." In that moment, the world he had left behind—of family warmth, of the gentle rhythm of home—felt suddenly, achingly near.

That small comfort became the final quiet preparation for the great ordeal ahead. The long months of negotiation, the battles over seating, etiquette, and currency—all had led to this. With his mother's words still echoing in his heart, Henry felt steadied, renewed, ready. The next morning, at nine o'clock, he would walk beside Townsend Harris through the gates of the Shogun's palace in Edo. There, in the inner sanctum of power unseen by any Westerner before, they would deliver the President's letter—an act that would mark the beginning of the end of Japan's two centuries of isolation. The ink on that letter, Henry knew, would do what no fleet of warships ever could: open the heart of an empire.

15

The Shogun and the Sword

The morning of December 7, 1857, was the fulcrum of history.

At precisely nine o'clock, Henry Heusken and Townsend Harris, preceded by the retinue of Shinano no Kami and followed by the Vice-Governor, moved through the silent, massive enclosures of the Imperial Castle. The walls, the layered gates, and the final moat were designed to repel the world, and every step they took was a literal triumph over two centuries of isolation.

The final enclosure, the true Imperial Castle, was deceptively picturesque, adorned with white, three-storied pagodas and plastered galleries, all kept in splendid condition—a calculated display of serene strength. At the fourth bridge, Harris finally left his norimon, the final surrender to the palace's hierarchy, and they proceeded on foot through four more gates to the courtyard.

They exchanged their soiled shoes for new ones, an act of ritual purification, and climbed the seven steps into the Palace. In the antechamber, the Commissioners paid their respects, and one official, with surreal kindness, asked the Ambassador if he wished to visit the men's room. The immense political gravity of the moment was perpetually interrupted by the petty, human needs of protocol.

The Kneeling Throng

They were led through a great hall of soaring wooden pillars, past a screen, and finally, the command was given: the Taikun was on his throne. A profound, charged silence was enforced by a sound so well known throughout the world—the command for quiet.

Preceded by the two Ometsuke (now elevated to Masters of Ceremonies) and Shinano no Kami, the Ambassador entered, followed by Henry, who carried the President's letter wrapped in the American colors.

They passed through a crowd of six to seven hundred kneeling court nobles. These were the men who constituted the heart of the Shogunate's power, yet their posture was that of absolute servitude. They wore their court costume: a square-shaped lacquer cap perched atop their head, pale yellow hemp garments with wide sleeves, and trousers twice as long as the leg that dragged behind them, forcing them to shuffle and giving them the appearance of walking on their knees.

Despite the significant number of courtiers, the silence was most profound. The only weapons carried were scimitars, hidden in their silk belts—a final mark of their military-administrative caste.

The Man on the Stool

On reaching the inner partitioning, the Ometsuke and Shinano no Kami fell upon their knees, dragging themselves forward. Harris, walking upright, bowed and ascended one step, proceeding the length of two mats, bowing a second time, and a third on the fifth mat, where he halted.

Around him, the five members of the Great Council and five other dignitaries knelt, making themselves small before the ultimate source of power.

From Henry's position, the floor rose another step. The Taikun of Japan—Shogun Iesada—was seated on a stool on a platform about three feet high, at the rear of the chamber. The chamber was deliberately dark, and the curtain hanging from the ceiling hid his face.

Henry, standing erect, strained to see the monarch who held the fate of the Empire. The courtiers on their knees could see him clearly, but for the two standing Westerners, the sight was deliberately obscured.

Harris, the relentless man who had fought two years for this single moment, delivered the final, choreographed speech:

"May it please Your Majesty, in presenting my letters of credence from the President of the United States of America, I am directed to express to Your Majesty the sincere wishes of the President for your health and happiness and for the prosperity of your dominions…"

Upon the conclusion, the Shogun made a sound that Henry registered as stamping his feet three times, and answered in Japanese. The chief interpreter, Moriyama Takichiro, translated the reply in his native Dutch:

"Vergenoegd met eenen brief gezonden met the afgezant of een verafgelegen gewest and tenses met zyn gesprek. Eeuwig zal Gemeenschap gehouden worden."

(Pleased with the letter sent with the Ambassador from a far distant country, and likewise pleased with his discourse. The Intercourse shall be continued forever.)

It was a cold, formal statement, utterly devoid of the personal pronoun "I", because, as Henry noted, "the Taikun is too great to use the small word 'I'."

The Profanation

At the climax of the ceremony, Henry, who had waited at the entrance of the Imperial Chamber, advanced. Making the compulsory three bows, he presented the President's letter to Harris, who opened it, showed the President's signature to the Minister of Foreign Affairs, and handed it over. The Minister, in turn, placed it on a small table before the throne.

This single, silent act—the delivery of a letter from the head of an upstart republic to the descendant of Ieyasu, a monarch who had once mandated that anyone who carried a letter from abroad would be put to death with his entire family—shattered centuries of isolation.

Henry looked at the hundreds of kneeling courtiers, the Shogun obscured in the shadows, the simplicity of the court that eschewed the barbaric luxury of Siam for a noble and dignified bearing. He saw the confrontation clearly:

Not one sword is unsheathed; not one guardian of the throne among this legion of nobles rises to impede the progress of those two profaners; not one cry of sacrilege is heard.

The Court of Edo had not been struck powerless, but by the sun of civilization, the star of progress. The Shogunate, proud but pragmatic, had finally been forced to acknowledge the power of the peoples of the West.

Yet, Henry's triumph was laced with fear. He, who had admired the artlessness and simple customs of Japan, feared the fatal vices the Western people would bring. The abundance, the happy laughter of the children—all that happiness, he feared, was coming to an end.

The Taikun's Dinner

The ceremony concluded with the official exchange of gifts. Fifteen robes of silk were presented to Harris, and a separate, smaller present—also robes—was given to "Mr. Heusken." This recognition, however small, was a personal triumph for Henry.

After they had thanked the Shogun, Hotta announced, "His Majesty presents you a dinner."

They were led to an adjacent chamber where they dined, served on small tables made of plain wood—a great compliment, they were told, because the wooden plates and dishes were to be used only once for this dinner and afterwards be discarded. The Ambassadors' tables were adorned with paper figures representing Banzioe and Yakousin, persons who had lived more than 1,100 years—the Japanese "compliment of longevity."

Finally, after the feast, they returned to their residence in the same manner in which they had come, exchanging bows with the Ometsuke and the Great Council.

The great audience was complete. The Shogun had received the American Ambassador in the heart of the forbidden capital. Henry Heusken, the young American Diplomat, had been the indispensable key that unlocked the door to Dai Nippon. The isolation was irrevocably broken. The fate of the treaty, however, still hung in a delicate balance—its future now resting in the hands of the Great Council and upon the skill of Harris and Henry to guide events toward progress without igniting chaos. Their task was as perilous as it was historic: to secure Japan's opening to the world while avoiding the spark of a civil war that smoldered beneath the surface of the Shogunate's rigid order. Every word, every gesture, carried the weight of a nation's destiny—one false move, and diplomacy could give way to rebellion.

16

The Gilded Cage

The triumph of the Taikun audience dissolved immediately into the suffocating reality of the Edo residency as negotiations on the actual treaty slowly started. The palace apartment, though clean and equipped with Western conveniences, quickly felt like a gilded cage to Henry. The walls were thick with history, but they were also thick with guarded suspicion, cutting him off from the vibrant chaos of the million-souled capital he had fought so hard to enter.

Diplomatic work began on Tuesday, December 8, 1857. Harris, though exhausted, immediately asserted his presence, writing to the Minister of Foreign Affairs, Hotta, Bitchū no Kami, that he was ready to send his important communications to the Great Council. Courtesies followed: the Prince of Shinano was dispatched expressly to inquire after the Ambassador's health.

Henry used the enforced confinement for observation. He noted the high-ranking officials who came to inquire about Harris's health—men who represented the true axis of power in Japan. The Great Council, composed of men appointed by the Taikun since the usurpation of Ieyasu, wielded absolute

118

authority over three hundred hereditary princes and even the eighty ancient princes of the Empire. This was the fortress they had to breach.

The Anatomy of Surveillance

The initial clash was not over trade, but over trust.

Henry was stunned when Shinano no Kami, the Prince of Shinano, gravely informed them that the Great Council was deliberating over Harris's seemingly harmless request for two maps of Edo. What to Western eyes appeared an innocent scholarly inquiry was, in Japan, an act fraught with peril. Barely twenty years earlier, a Dutchman named Philipp Franz von Siebold had obtained two maps of Japan from the Director of the Imperial School of Astronomy. When the court discovered that these maps had left the country, the director was condemned to the most severe punishment imaginable—crucifixion—for the crime of betraying state secrets.

In that chilling moment, Henry grasped the depth of Japan's isolationist paranoia: here, knowledge itself was treason, and curiosity could be a death sentence. The law was not a shield of justice but a weapon of control—personal, absolute, and terrifyingly arbitrary. What Harris had considered a routine diplomatic request had become a matter of life and death within the walls of Edo's silent bureaucracy.

The presence of spies, whom Harris had temporarily defeated in Shimoda, was now reinforced in the capital. A multitude of officers from Edo were quartered at their residence, and the very same spies who were shamefully expelled from Shimoda had their quarters near the entrance gate. Everything that entered or left their residence was subjected to inspection.

Henry witnessed the anguish of the polite Japanese officers firsthand. They were extremely polite when observed, but privately, they would apologize to Henry, their voices low with fear. They had to maintain a haughty distance from the foreigner because the house was full of spies, and any hint of friendship would have fatal consequences for them.

Harris, burdened by a profound sense of isolation, realized he could no longer endure his current circumstances. His frustration and anger were further compounded by a recurring illness that had plagued him since his arrival; he had never truly regained his strength or the weight he had lost during those first grueling months in Japan. These bouts of physical suffering placed an immense strain on his temperament, and there is little doubt that when his health faltered, his patience with the Japanese officials would thin, occasionally leading him to adopt a much harsher tone in his negotiations.

On Friday, December 11, 1857, he delivered his ultimatum to Shinano: Harris designated himself their prisoner and would not leave his house until the spies were immediately expelled. He declared the surveillance an insult to the honor of the President he represented, stating the entire affair was a sufficient reason for the United States to declare war on Japan.

Poor Shinano was visibly embarrassed, caught between the unforgiving Council and the volatile American. He beseeched Harris to attend the conference with the Minister tomorrow, pleading that his position was at stake—a clear allusion to *harakiri*. Harris finally yielded, but only on the condition that the matter would be satisfactorily settled afterwards.

The Sublime Moment of Conscience

The truce held, and on Saturday, December 12, 1857, Harris and Henry went to the palace of the Prime Minister, Hotta, Bitchū no Kami, for the conference that seemed much more important than the audience with the Taikun.

The scene was one of contained power. Moriyama and Tsunenosuke knelt, motionless, their heads low, their posture a mirror of the imperial edicts that governed every soul in the chamber.

Harris seized the moment to deliver his comprehensive vision. It was a sublime moment when he touched on the forbidden topic of religion. It was the first time, since the cruel persecutions had succeeded in crushing Christianity, that a voice had raised itself in favor of the persecuted religion within the highest political chamber of the Empire. Henry felt the weight of the words.

The Imperial Edict of 1688—the law promising five hundred pieces of silver for the discovery of a priest and threatening death to those who propagated the faith—was still in force. Yet, as Harris spoke of the freedom of conscience, the Minister of Foreign Affairs showed not a sign of displeasure. The terrifying word Christianity, the phantom that undermined the dynasty of Ieyasu, failed to bring the slightest cloud to his peaceful features.

It is worth noting that from the very day Harris and Henry arrived in Japan, they had steadfastly refused to work or receive visitors on Sundays. From the beginning, they made it clear that this holy day was sacred to them—a private boundary amid the ceaseless demands of diplomacy. Each Sunday, whether confined within the consulate at Shimoda or later in Edo, the two men would hold a quiet service together, reading scripture and praying in the stillness of their isolation. These small, steadfast observances became an anchor for both, a reminder of faith and home in a land where neither was easily found. For Harris and Henry, the freedom to worship was as essential as the freedom to trade—both acts of conscience that defined their mission and their sense of purpose in the heart of a closed empire.

Thus, when Harris spoke to the Prime Minister that day, his words had to be meticulously measured. He stressed that the era of the Spanish and Portuguese—a time defined by a cruel and lawless method of spreading religion through a combination of a lust for gold and the edge of a sword—was finally over. Thus, Harris stressed:

"Mankind has finally learned that freedom of conscience is the great principle that should govern all nations, and in America one can see a temple of Buddha rising next to a Christian Church."

Henry imagined he heard a hymn of praise intoned by the sacrificed martyrs of Shimabara, their long-silenced voices echoing through this historic concession. The Shogunate, bound by pragmatic necessity, found itself forced to listen to Harris's advocacy for compassion and religious freedom. However, this diplomatic tolerance had strict limits; it did not mean the Japanese authorities were prepared to permit Christians to practice their faith openly or to attempt the conversion of the Japanese people.

Commerce and Catastrophe

Harris pressed on with calm conviction, extolling the advantages of free trade—an idea the Japanese regarded as mercenary, almost beneath the dignity of the Empire. Yet Harris, ever the diplomat, turned the argument to their pride. A nation as brave and industrious as Japan, he said, should not allow foreigners alone to profit from the vast resources of the seas. Why should the courageous Japanese not send their own ships to the distant coasts of America and claim a share of the whaling trade for themselves?

His words, translated fluently by Henry, found their mark. The Minister listened with polite attentiveness, even smiling, and assured them that the matter would be faithfully transmitted to the Great Council for deliberation.

After the meeting, councilors withdrew to consider their reply, leaving Harris and Henry to wait in anxious limbo. The weeks that followed were slow and heavy, filled with diplomatic silence. To escape the confines of the residence, Henry was permitted occasional rides to a broad square atop a nearby hill, where he could look out over the vast sprawl of Edo, its tiled roofs and smoky haze stretching to the horizon. There, in brief moments of freedom, he could almost forget the tension of their mission—until nature itself reminded him of Japan's volatility.

Shaking in the New Year

The closing months of 1857 and the dawn of 1858 were marked by a near-constant trembling beneath Edo's streets. Earthquakes seemed to strike daily, as if the very gods were shaking the earth in protest—or in preparation—for the changes to come. It felt, perhaps, as though nature itself resisted the efforts of Harris and Henry as they pressed forward in their mission to open Japan to the world.

That Christmas, the two men spent the holiday quietly in their residence—likely the first to celebrate the Christian holy day in Edo. Yet the gift they most desired was not one wrapped in paper and ribbon, but a reply from the Shogunate: an answer to their proposals. Still, even in Edo, within reach of the shogun's court, decisions came slowly. Every matter of consequence, they were told, must first be weighed by the Tycoon's brothers, the great daimyō, and other high ministers. Letters would be written, responses exchanged, and deliberations stretched on without end. Thus, no message arrived for Henry or Harris that Christmas of 1857—no acknowledgment, no progress, only silence and waiting.

New Year's Eve brought yet another earthquake, a fitting close to a year of unrest. But New Year's Day offered a moment of reflection. Harris, his health failing and his strength uncertain, gave thanks to Almighty God for allowing him to see the beginning of another year. Henry, watching his older companion—past fifty and visibly weary—could not promise himself that Harris would live to see the next. Together, they looked back with quiet pride at what they had accomplished for the honor of the United States and looked ahead with hope that the coming year might finally bring Japan's full opening to the world.

On that New Year's Day, they received visitors: the Princes of Tōke and Shinano, who came in full ceremonial dress, bearing small gifts in honor of the occasion. Their conversation was pleasant and courteous, though carefully devoid of business. For one day, at least, diplomacy yielded to civility—and amid the trembling earth and the long wait for change, Henry and Harris found a brief, fragile peace.

On January 2, 1858, the largest of the quakes struck, and the ground beneath Henry suddenly heaved with a deep, undulating motion that lasted for nearly half a minute. The earthquake rattled the city and his nerves alike, a violent echo of the great disaster two years earlier that had reduced a sixth of Edo to ruins. It was as if the very earth shared the unrest of the nation above it.

The long silence finally broke on January 16, 1858, when Hotta, Prince of Bitchū, arrived bearing the government's long-awaited response. The message was momentous: the Shogunate agreed in principle to free trade and accepted the proposal for a resident American minister, though the specifics of timing and location were left open for further negotiation. For Harris and Henry, who had endured months of uncertainty, it was a breakthrough—but also the beginning of a far greater challenge.

Two days later, on January 18, 1858, the formal exchange of full powers took place. In a solemn ceremony rich with ritual, the two Americans—representatives of a young, distant republic—received the red-sealed commissions of the Shogun's appointed negotiators: Inoue, Prince of Shinano, and Iwase, Prince of Higo. With the exchange complete, the draft treaty was formally presented. The diplomatic match had entered its decisive phase. The framework was established, but the real struggle—the intricate battle over each article, and the inevitable clash with the powerful daimyō opposition—still lay ahead.

Yet amid the solemnity and purpose of their mission, some moments struck both men as strangely absurd. On January 20, 1858, Harris received a letter from Mr. Rice, the U.S. Commercial Agent stationed in Hakodate, who was responsible for assisting American whaling ships entering port. His message was startlingly blunt—he demanded that "women must and will be provided" for the U.S. sailors when they came ashore.

The request bordered on the ridiculous, and it is difficult to imagine either Harris or Henry taking such a demand seriously. Still, the letter served as an unintended reminder of the broader consequences of opening Japan to the outside world. The exchange of commerce and diplomacy was one thing, but with it came the less noble impulses of human behavior—realities that neither Harris nor Henry, in their idealism, may have fully anticipated.

17

The Loo-Nin Plot

The immense political energy unleashed by the Americans was contained within the small, sterile room of the Great Council. Here, Henry Heusken translated the clash between the West's ruthless pursuit of commerce and the East's rigid defense of tradition. The pace was glacial, demanding patience—a necessity in a land where progress came in small, careful steps rather than bold leaps.

On Monday, January 25, 1858, the negotiations began in earnest, with the Commissioners—Iwase, Prince of Higo, and Inoue, Prince of Shinano—voicing the deep-seated fears of the Shogunate.

The key points of resistance were not trivial; they were the foundation of Japanese control. Harris demanded that a diplomatic minister must reside in Edo, the capital, calling any compromise a dishonor to the United States. The Commissioners countered, pleading that they must account for public opinion, which remained prejudiced against foreigners, particularly among the powerful Daimyos and the military.

The Floating Menace

Then, the threat became personal. The diplomatic pressure yielded to the cold reality of assassination.

The Commissioners spoke of the rōh-nin—men floating upon the water—the masterless samurai, younger sons of officials abandoned by their families. These vagabonds, driven by a lack of purpose and a samurai's ingrained desire for glory, were the government's most lethal liability.

"Three of these men have been arrested recently," they confessed, their voices low. "They had plotted to do harm to the Ambassador of the United States."

Henry felt a chill. The government, in great uneasiness, claimed their guards were there because the American household could hardly sleep for fear of an attack. The implication was chilling: if the Americans demanded the right to travel throughout the Empire, they would expose themselves to accidents that might have fatal consequences.

Townsend Harris, the Puritan elder, met the raw threat with serene moral superiority. He was not in the least afraid, he asserted, and was eternally grateful for their solicitude. Then, he performed a masterful stroke of diplomacy, transforming the threat into a testament to American benevolence.

Harris requested pardons for the three rōh-nins as a favor. He argued that his mission was one of peace and friendship, and that clemency often proved more effective than severity in preventing future crimes. He was turning the Shogunate's fear of its own people into a public-relations coup—a demonstration of the compassionate superiority of Western law. The request was transmitted, though the Commissioners quickly noted that the rōh-nin had not injured Harris, but the government of Japan, since they were plotting to harm the Shogun's guests, and thus the Shogun retained the right to punish them.

The Siege of Residence and Trade

The negotiations dragged on with an almost ritualized intensity, every point contested, every phrase weighed as if it were a matter of life and death. The Japanese negotiators, bound by centuries of precedent and terror of internal upheaval, yielded only under the relentless pressure of Harris's cold, methodical logic, sharpened by Henry's deft translations. Each concession was extracted inch by inch, the Shogunate's fear of change clashing with Harris's conviction that the opening of Japan was not merely a diplomatic act, but a moral inevitability.

On matters of currency and residence, the Japanese clung desperately to old systems. In 1850, Japan utilized a dual-track monetary system that balanced a traditional feudal economy and one for international trade. Official currency functioned under a "metallic standard," consisting of gold, silver, and copper coins minted by the central Shogunate for high-level trade and government accounting. Conversely, regional commerce relied on "fiduciary" paper money known as hansatsu, which were notes issued by individual local lords and backed by their own credit or rice reserves. This complex structure meant that while metal coins were recognized nationwide, the paper money was typically only valid within the specific domain where it was issued. Thus, the Japanese refused to permit the free circulation of foreign coins, insisting instead on the use of their own paper money, a compromise that symbolized their reluctance to let the foreign world infiltrate their economy.

Even more contentious was the issue of residence. The government demanded that Americans be confined to designated, segregated quarters—tiny enclaves meant to contain the contamination of foreign influence. It was, Henry realized, the architecture of isolation rebuilt in miniature: comforting to the Japanese, but fatally outdated.

The "family barrier" proved even more telling. The Shogunate balked at allowing American wives and children to live in Edo, fearing that the presence of families implied permanence. A foreign colony within the capital was not just a diplomatic concern—it was a symbolic invasion of the domestic sanctum that underpinned Japan's entire political order. To defend the home, in Japanese thought, was to defend the state itself.

At last came the debate over the travel clause—a seemingly minor issue that revealed the entire psychological battleground between the two sides. The Japanese, desperate to maintain some illusion of control, insisted that the Consul-General's movements within Japan be limited strictly to "official business." Yet the phrase itself was a masterstroke of ambiguity. What, after all, counted as official business? Harris, with his characteristic blend of precision and irony, was already prepared to interpret the term broadly. If he chose to climb Mount Fujiyama for the sake of his health—or his spirit—he could, with perfect dignity, declare it an act of official duty. In that subtle play of language, Harris had secured not merely the right to travel, but the quiet freedom to define his own authority.

The articles on currency, freedom of movement, and residence were all crucial, but trade remained the heart of the treaty—the keystone upon which every other concession rested. This was, above all, a treaty of commerce, and its success depended on convincing the Japanese that trade was not a humiliation but a necessity. To Harris and Henry, commerce was the lifeblood of modern nations—the force that connected distant peoples through mutual benefit rather than conquest. Yet to the Japanese, bound by centuries of isolation, trade still carried the stench of corruption and loss of dignity. The challenge before them was not merely to negotiate terms, but to redefine what commerce meant in the eyes of an empire that had spent hundreds of years closing its gates to the world.

Harris fought them with philosophical elegance, arguing that the Daimyos' resistance was rooted in a profound misunderstanding of commerce itself—the fundamental error of confusing value with morality. He countered the Japanese view of trade as a venal objective with a sublime vision:

The True Purpose of Trade

Henry translated the words with deliberate force, watching the Commissioners, who were accustomed to viewing the merchant as the lowest rung of society, recoil from the foreign calculus. Harris was not advocating for individual profit, but for the existential health of the state.

"Your Excellencies," Harris stated, his voice quiet but commanding, "you see commerce as a sordid pursuit—a way to fill the coffers of a few individuals. This is not the whole truth. Trade is not a venal objective; it is conducive to a higher, more sublime purpose."

He shifted the argument from individual gain to national survival: "You speak of strength and dignity. Then look to history. Commerce is the blood, the great source of life of an empire."

Henry elaborated, translating Harris's precise historical comparisons. "Consider the nations. Look at England. It is a small island of fog and rock. Yet, what has made it the mightiest country in the world? Trade! Look at Holland, a land scarcely taken from the sea. What has made it a nation worthy of esteem? Trade! Without this exchange, this circulation of the economic blood, the people who live in those small countries would starve. Trade gives power and population."

He then delivered the fatal warning, the consequence of resisting this universal law: "For more than two hundred years, Spain and Portugal were the most powerful nations of the world. Now they enjoy a mediocre position. Why? Because they neglected trade! They mistook the pursuit of foreign gold for the internal health of industry. I implore you, adopt the course of Holland and England, and prevent Japan from becoming Spain and Portugal—nations whose pride led to stagnation."

Harris paused, allowing Henry's translation to settle.

Then he stressed Harri's words, "The President has not sent me here to steal your gold or throw money into the pockets of certain individuals. He sent me to paint to you the dangers which menace Japan and to propose the means for avoiding them. This commerce is the necessary antidote to foreign aggression, a way to build a large revenue by which you may support a respectable navy. It is the life, the great activity of nations, and if Japan is opened, there is no reason why it would not end in a most fortunate condition—the England of Asia."

Henry watched the Commissioners shift on their cushions. They were not convinced of the morality, but they were terrified by the historical inevitability Harris had described.

The Fight for Osaka

As negotiations turned to the question of commerce, the most delicate issue arose: which ports would Japan open to American ships? The Japanese officials understood all too well that opening a harbor to one foreign power meant inevitably opening it to all. Once the Americans were granted access, the British, French, and Russians would soon follow, each demanding the same rights under the banner of equality.

The decision, therefore, required more than diplomacy—it demanded foresight. The Shogunate had to choose its ports with strategic precision, balancing the need to satisfy Harris's demands without exposing the country's vulnerable coastline to a flood of foreign influence.

Thus, the most crucial battle centered on the ports of Osaka and Miyako (Kyoto). The Japanese asserted that Miyako—the seat of the Mikado, the spiritual head of Nippon—was too sacred, a source of potential rebellion.

Harris compromised, asking for Osaka instead, only three ri from the holy city. The Japanese immediately offered Sakai, three ri away from Osaka, with the cruel, restrictive condition that Americans could only go to Osaka during the day to transact business, and must return to Sakai at night.

Harris launched his final, withering attack. He asked what would happen if an American merchant became ill in Osaka and the sun set?

"You would do better to close the city completely than to say: 'You may be here in the daytime, but you are too vile, too low to be permitted to sleep within our walls.' You treat Americans like lepers."

This fierce moral outrage ultimately forced the Shogunate's hand. By Monday, February 8, 1858, they conceded to open Osaka for residence and commerce in 1863, one year after the scheduled opening of Edo. In their desperation to avoid the concept of "permanent" residence and appease the wary Daimyos, they ironically proposed a clause that granted the very access they feared: "these places will be opened for the residence and commerce of Americans." Crucially, they omitted the word "permanent," a linguistic sleight of hand intended to soothe domestic opposition while legally providing Harris with the foothold he required.

Harris and Henry had wrested from the Council a formal agreement, yet the Council alone could not enact it. Final ratification required the assent of the Shogun himself. Still, the breakthrough felt monumental. Article by article, the treaty seemed to have been won, secured through relentless patience, precise strategy, and Harris's unshakeable moral authority. Even the most cautious Japanese officials, in a rare display of concession, confirmed their intention to send an ambassador to Washington to exchange ratifications—a symbolic acknowledgment that the door, closed to foreigners for centuries, might at last swing both ways.

Yet the treaty remained unsigned, a fragile construct suspended between hope and danger. The political atmosphere in Edo was intensely volatile. Isolationist Daimyos whispered against concessions, conservative courtiers fretted over precedent, and the Shogunate itself teetered under pressure from multiple factions. For all the victories achieved at the negotiating table, the ultimate fate of the treaty—and of Japan's first steps toward opening to the world—hung by a thread, poised between diplomacy and potential crisis.

18

The European Hammer

The Daimyo revolt was no longer a fear—it was a fact. On Wednesday, February 17, 1858, the Great Council, reeling from the fury of the isolationist lords, confessed their defeat in the diplomatic chamber.

Prime Minister Hotta, Bitchū no Kami, had summoned the feudal princes and informed them of the concessions Harris had won—the resident minister, the open ports, the sanctity of the American word. The result was great confusion and outright refusal. The majority of Daimyo would not give their approval, risking open civil war.

"We have no regard for life; it does not matter to us," they had proclaimed, their subjects—tens of thousands of warriors— sharing their fanaticism. "But we wish to remain faithful to the ancient laws of our ancestors."

The Shogunate, unable to suppress this domestic rebellion, resorted to a spiritual gambit. They would delay the signing and send a member of the Great Council to Miyako (Kyoto) to demand the concurrence of the Mikado, the spiritual leader of the Empire. This Mikado Gambit was a cynical attempt to use religious superstition as leverage against the secular anger of the Daimyo.

Henry, translating the sheer desperation of their plan, noted the enormous timeline: two months minimum, and if the Mikado "makes objections" (a possibility the Commissioners dismissed with political bravado), the treaty would die.

Townsend Harris, who had suffered in the gilded cage for months, knew a delay meant failure. The long-feared European fleets, fresh from the devastation of China, were already gathering. He was not threatening war; he was predicting a catastrophe.

Harris replied that it was unprecedented in diplomacy to negotiate a treaty without signing it. He offered a compromise: the government could keep the signing secret, but he could not accept indefinite delay. While he could not force the Commissioners to sign, he would continue pressing unresolved points.

The Commissioners then raised minor objections—first regarding the Fifteenth Article on sending diplomatic agents, then over terminology, suggesting "high officer" instead of "consular agent" since the Japanese language lacked the term. Harris quickly saw their tactic: prolonging negotiations by quibbling over words, likely to delay or observe developments before committing.

The Unshakable Logic

On Thursday, February 18, 1858, Harris dispatched a note to Shinano no Kami, demanding a private meeting. He confessed the personal toll of the siege—"I cannot remain any longer in Edo, that I will die of it,"—a truth both personal and diplomatic. He needed to escape the city, but he would not leave the treaty behind.

He laid out his final, unanswerable argument, appealing not to friendship but to survival. The threat of the European powers—England and France—was the ultimate lever.

Harris had spent the preceding weeks relentlessly drilling officials on the necessity of the treaty as a shield against predatory foreign powers. He argued that a treaty of commerce would serve as a vital defense against European nations, whom he portrayed as being intent on conquest rather than the equitable trading partnership sought by the United States. Harris posited a reciprocal vision: as Japan opened its doors to Americans, the United States would, in turn, open its doors to Japan, fostering a truly mutually beneficial relationship. He warned that if the Europeans were permitted to force a treaty first, the terms would undoubtedly be one-sided and exploitative. However, by establishing a precedent with the Americans, Japan could effectively compel European powers to adopt similar, balanced terms. Ultimately, Harris's message was blunt: the United States stood as a friend, while the Europeans would arrive only as conquerors.

The Japanese Commissioners knew he was right. Moriyama, the interpreter, confessed that the actual danger from the Daimyo lies in the significant concessions, but admitted, "We understand nothing about commerce, and we are compelled to believe you who have assured us, on your honor, that those regulations are for the welfare of Japan."

The government was caught between the calamity from within (civil war) and the catastrophe from outside (foreign invasion).

Harris's Final Compromise

Harris offered the Shogunate a lifeline—a way to save face with the Daimyo while ensuring the treaty remained secure against the looming threat of European pressure. On Thursday, February 18, 1858, he proposed a clever compromise: the treaty would be finalized and copied, every detail prepared for signatures, but it would not yet be signed.

Henry translated the plan with precision: the treaty would be fully agreed upon and copied, Hotta would send Harris a letter acknowledging its readiness but citing "important reasons" (the Mikado Gambit) to postpone the formal signing, Harris would return to Shimoda to complete his dispatches and wait, and when the Japanese government deemed it appropriate, they would send a steamship to bring him back to Edo for the signing. The government accepted the proposal the next day.

It was a tactical masterstroke: the Daimyo could be told the treaty remained unsigned, preserving their honor, while the finalized document was safely secured, shielding Japan from the possibility of harsher European demands. Even the Prince of Kaga, chief of the most powerful Daimyo and a vocal opponent who had declared it "better to fight immediately than to consent to such things," was temporarily placated.

The Last Words

The final days were spent in a race against time, copying and verifying the final clauses. Henry noted the absurd, continuous arguments the Commissioners raised, even over grammatical articles—Moriyama arguing that the Dutch article *de* could mean *all* places, a desperate, last-ditch effort to keep a loophole open.

The Japanese, however, did not flinch on the core demands: the great Daimyos—the Prince of Kaga and the Prince of Satsuma—refused entry to anyone into their territories. The treaty was thus modified: only the Ambassador/Consul-General would be permitted to travel everywhere, as their higher rank afforded them inviolability. The ordinary Consul, being a lower official, would be restricted.

This was the final, complex reality. The doors were open, but Japan's political map remained fiercely protected. The Shogun had yielded to Harris, but the powerful regional lords remained hostile, armed, and ready to fight for the path of their ancestors.

The treaty was ready. The decision was final. Henry Heusken had done his part. Now, Henry and his mentor had to survive the perilous journey out of Edo and wait for the signal that would call them back to sign the end of one era and the beginning of another.

19

The Fever and the Father

The diplomatic triumph of finalizing the treaty—Harris's crowning achievement—was immediately shadowed by a sudden and terrifying collapse. On Saturday, February 27, 1858, the unflinching Consul-General, the man who had faced Daimyo, navigated labyrinthine protocol, and endured months of harsh winter confinement in Edo, was struck down. Henry discovered him wracked with fever, vomiting, and complaining of an agonizing headache, every bone in his body aching as if the weight of months of relentless exertion had finally settled upon him.

The indefatigable force who had driven both men tirelessly through the trials of diplomacy now had nothing left to give. Harris himself, once resolute to the point of stubbornness, had written that remaining in Edo could very well cost him his life—and it seemed that grim warning was coming to pass. The room, usually charged with the energy of their mission, was now filled with the silent, urgent tension of a crisis that threatened not just a man, but the fragile momentum of Japan's opening to the world.

The Heir Apparent

With Hotta, Bitchū no Kami, preparing to travel to Miyako to win the Mikado's blessing, the negotiations could not pause. On Monday, March 1, 1858, with Harris confined to his bed in Edo, the ultimate responsibility fell squarely onto Henry's shoulders.

The Prince of Shinano, grave and solicitous, arrived at the residence. Henry, alone, received him.

"I receive him alone," Henry scribbled, the sheer, terrifying weight of the sentence marking his transition from secretary to plenipotentiary in fact.

Shinano, acutely aware of Harris's weakened state, seized the opportunity to raise a flurry of objections to the treaty articles, despite the agreement being ostensibly finalized. With Harris confined to his bed, gravely ill, it seemed the Japanese might try to intimidate and push Henry around. Yet Henry, drawing upon every lesson his mentor had drilled into him over months of relentless diplomacy, stood firm. Armed with flawless translations and the indomitable authority of Harris's earlier instructions, the young diplomat became the sole barrier holding the Shogunate at bay. On Tuesday, March 2, 1978, he faced the Commissioners again, allowing only minor, inconsequential changes. Gradually, the Japanese yielded: the treaty was officially concluded, and a final copy could be written. The work was done.

Yet the triumph was shadowed by an urgent peril. Harris, though victorious in the intricate battles of negotiation and persuasion, was losing the most personal and critical fight of all—he was rapidly succumbing to illness. The war of diplomacy had been won, but the war for Harris's very life was just beginning.

The Snowbound Escape

On Friday, March 5, 1858, Harris had grown so frail that the oppressive isolation of Edo became unbearable. Desperate for the spiritual sanctuary of their old consulate, he demanded an immediate return to Shimoda. "Mr. Harris feels so ill that he asks me to propose to the government that the steamer take him to Shimoda today, and that I would come when the other copies are ready," Henry recorded, conveying the palpable urgency in his mentor's voice. To facilitate this, they opted for the sea route back to Shimoda; although it covered a longer distance than the overland journey, the steamer provided a far quicker and less physically demanding passage for a man in Harris's precarious state of health.

Even in the shadow of possible death, Harris performed one final act of diplomatic foresight. He signed the two completed copies of the treaty, ensuring that a record could be sent to Washington should any "accident" befall him. Henry carefully bound the documents and affixed the seal of the United States in Harris's presence—a solemn acknowledgment that the work of years was now protected, even if its author might not survive to witness its triumph.

The next day, Saturday, March 6, their departure was a scene of chaos and desperation. A relentless snowfall blanketed Edo as Henry lifted his mentor from the norimon at the embarcadero and physically supported him onto the waiting launch. "I lift him from the norimon and put him in the boat," he wrote simply, though the act carried the weight of profound responsibility. The father figure, the indomitable man of iron will and unyielding principle, had been reduced to a helpless passenger, wholly dependent on the courage and strength of his apprentice.

After a harrowing, freezing night voyage, they reached Shimoda. Henry once again bore Harris from the landing at Kakizaki to the consulate, as the Consul-General could barely walk. At last, they retreated into Gyokusenji Temple—no longer a place of confinement, but a sanctuary. Here, in this temporary refuge, the true crisis began: the battle for Harris's life had just begun, even as the fruits of his years of labor glimmered within reach.

The Care of the Soul

In the days that followed, at the U.S. Consulate, now their sanctuary within Gyokusenji Temple, Harris's condition worsened with alarming speed. His once-commanding presence had been reduced to agonized moans, and he fell from his bed, crying out in despair: "Assist me. I am lame." The proud, unyielding Consul-General, who had faced the full weight of a centuries-old empire with unshakable resolve, now confronted a far more merciless adversary: his own failing body.

The Japanese Governor of Shimoda, moved by genuine concern, offered the services of the physician who had accompanied him to Edo. Harris refused, as if to deny that even the assistance of a doctor could intrude upon his dignity. Stoicism clung to him even in torment, but his body betrayed him.

The Japanese doctors, called in despite his refusal, would later determine that he was stricken by a rheumatic disorder of the intestines, compounded by a nervous fever. Henry watched with mounting horror as brown blotches first appeared on Harris's legs, followed by deep purple spots. He recorded the word with a shudder: rot.

Each mark seemed to etch itself into the young diplomat's mind as a cruel reminder that the man who had bent an empire to diplomacy was now at the mercy of a disease that acknowledged no treaties or authority. The consulate, once a center of strategy and negotiation, had become a theater of human vulnerability, where courage and intellect were powerless against the ravages of illness.

Henry remained at his mentor's side, the weight of responsibility pressing down on him. The man who had taught him to confront emperors and Daimyos now relied entirely on his pupil's strength, and the shadow of mortality loomed over the fragile sanctuary they had fought so hard to secure.

Harris was fading fast. His mind, once as sharp and unyielding as the steel of his convictions, now wavered; he scarcely recognized Henry. The stone walls of Gyokusenji Temple, so long a refuge and a prison, now enclosed Henry alone, trembling with fear, forced to act entirely on his own authority. Against Harris's previous strict orders, he summoned a doctor and administered medicine, every motion weighted with dread and responsibility.

It was in the oppressive darkness of the temple, amidst the shadows of tatami mats and flickering lanterns, that their bond crystallized. Overcome by emotion, Henry leaned close to his fevered mentor and cried out, "Mr. Harris, would you not pray to God?" For a moment, Harris's ravaged mind misunderstood, hearing "pay" instead of "pray," and the faintest flicker of confusion crossed his features. But then, with an almost imperceptible yielding, he allowed Henry to read the prayers. In a voice faint but resolute, Harris murmured "Amen" at each pause, each syllable a testament to his enduring dignity.

Henry, inspired by the intensity of the moment, read on, tears streaming freely down his face. And in that desperate intimacy, he confessed his fear, the weight of his charge, and asked if Harris had anything to say. The answer came not in grand words or elaborate reflections, but in the stark, unadorned simplicity of a life fully lived:

"Mr. Heusken, I have no secrets. I have always led a life of great simplicity. I have never been encumbered with many estates. I am ready to see my God… The cloth that is here you may keep or give away… I always thought of making a will."

When Henry could no longer restrain his tears, Harris offered his final, unscripted blessing, spoken with the faint, weathered authority of a father and mentor:

"Heusken, wipe your nose not so near my face. Heusken, you are a good boy and a true friend. I leave the care of my soul to you."

In that moment, Henry Heusken ceased to be merely the secretary. He became the Ambassador's nurse, his confessor, and his spiritual heir. He had fulfilled his duties to the mission; now he fulfilled the far weightier duty to the man who had given him a new life, a new purpose.

20

The Unsigned Treaty

The temple compound at Kakizaki, once a prison, had become a refuge. After days of wrestling with death, the immense, unyielding spirit of Townsend Harris began to prevail.

On Saturday, March 13, 1858, the crisis passed. Henry, exhausted but profoundly relieved, watched his mentor awaken to the world. Harris's first act was a defiant assertion of his old self: he demanded the barber, refused to wait, and was discovered by Henry shaving himself with a razor. Clean linen, a full bath—the transformation was complete.

"I believe the danger is passed," Henry noted in his journal. Harris, leaning on the young man for support, walked to the entrance, contemplated nature for a few moments, and whispered: "I thank God now, since to see nature is to see Him."

The man of simple, profound faith and unshakeable will was restored. The father figure was back, but he was forever changed. He had confessed his life's simplicity and entrusted his soul to Henry, solidifying a bond that transcended diplomatic rank.

The Urgency of the Mission

Harris's recovery was swift, fueled by an almost manic focus on the unfinished treaty. His illness had been a severe setback, but it had not been a defeat. The Governor of Shimoda and his Vice-Governor, deeply concerned, continued their visits, bearing gifts from the Taikun—a box of sugar and one hundred eggs—and the spiritual offering of the "shita ni iro" (kneel down) procession for the Imperial present itself. This constant, high-level attention underscored the mission's importance: the Shogunate desperately needed Harris to return.

The Emperor had sent a present and a letter, delivered by Wakana, informing Harris that the Taikun had been informed of his illness and wished him well.

But the courtesies could not mask the political reality: the treaty, finalized by Henry and the Commissioners, was still unsigned by Japan, waiting for the return of the Prime Minister, Hotta, Bitchū no Kami, from his Mikado Gambit in Kyoto.

Harris refused to waste a moment. By Thursday, March 18, he felt strong enough to write to the Governor, declaring his intention to return to Edo by April 2. The fate of Japan, he knew, could not wait for a full recovery.

The War of Dates

The Japanese, still fearing the volatile Daimyo factions, immediately resisted the early departure. On Wednesday, April 7, 1858, the Governor visited Harris in person.

The official line was solicitous: the doctors, sent by the government, claimed it was dangerous for him to travel. They urged him not to leave before May 13. The underlying political fear was transparent: Hotta had not yet returned from Kyoto, and the signing was contingent on the success of his mission to win the Mikado's sanction.

Harris, the old hand, saw the political maneuver instantly. He showed the Governor the letter from Hotta, which promised the treaty would be signed in two months—a deadline that was rapidly expiring.

Harris would not postpone his departure for a single day. The delay was no longer a question of health; it was a matter of political survival. They had escaped the rōh-nin threat, but the arrival of the European fleet was a far greater, unpreventable danger. Harris had to be in Edo when the Europeans arrived, treaty in hand, ready to act as Japan's protector.

The confrontation was tense. The Governor, pleading for a delay of even one week, could not break Harris's iron will. The American now set the date. Edo, regardless of the Daimyos, the Mikado, or the weather, would receive them.

Henry, watching his mentor, realized that the mission was about to enter its final, critical phase. The struggle for the treaty was no longer confined to the council chamber; it was now a race against the European Hammer and a desperate political gamble against the very forces of tradition they were attempting to save. The unsigned treaty, the paper shield against global conquest, was still vulnerable, and Henry Heusken was ready to support the final, decisive move.

21

The Second Coming

The diplomatic window was closing. Harris, physically restored but consumed by the singular fire of his mission, set the date for their return: April 15, 1858. The duo of diplomacy prepared to journey back to the very furnace of power, Edo, where the fate of the treaty—and the price of their lives—would finally be determined.

The return trip was a comic opera of incompetence and desperation, a perfect reflection of the Shogunate's uneven grasp on modernity. Harris insisted on immediate departure, only for the Japanese steamer captain to confess that he knew nothing of tacking about, yielding to the tide and wind, forcing them to return to Shimoda. They tried again the next day, only to be struck by a squall that sent the captain into a panic, forcing him to put about three times in frantic confusion.

The Japanese, Henry noted wryly, were masters of philosophy and paper architecture, but beginners in the cruel science of steam and sea. The journey that should have taken a day dragged into three, punctuated by hesitant stops in small bays like Ajiro and Uraga.

At Uraga, where the sea was "most serene," the captain's final act of caution was to refuse to proceed to Shinagawa before nightfall, claiming the bay was dangerous. Henry, desperate for solid ground and a break from the suffocating steamer, tried to go ashore, only to be blocked by the Vice-Governor, who had to ask the Governor's permission.

"I state that I do not wish to go ashore after the Governor's permission. I will go immediately or not at all."

The small victory was enough. On Sunday, April 18, 1858, they finally arrived at Shinagawa.

The Price of the Mikado Gambit

The second entrance into the capital was subdued. They caused much less sensation than before. The awe had faded, replaced by the grim familiarity of an occupied territory. Moriyama, the Shogun's reliable interpreter, received them with magnificent gifts from the leader—lovely potted flowers and a dwarf cherry tree—cultural balm to soothe the inevitable political news.

The news arrived swiftly on Monday, April 19, 1858. Shinano no Kami delivered a letter from Prime Minister Hotta, who was still in Kyoto. The mission to win the Mikado's sanction had failed. Hotta cannot keep his promise to have the treaty signed on the appointed date.

The Mikado's refusal was the ultimate escalation. It meant the treaty was now a tool for the anti-foreign Daimyo faction, who could claim the Shogun was defying the sacred authority of the Son of Heaven. The political crisis was no longer a matter of protocol; it was a crisis of state legitimacy. The delay was no longer temporary; it was a reprieve for rebellion.

Henry knew that every day they remained in Edo, the rōh-nin and the fierce, xenophobic factions were mobilizing. The city, outwardly serene, was a tinderbox, its fuse lit by the Mikado's veto.

The Mystery of the Fan

Amidst the stifling political tension, Henry found a necessary respite in the exquisite, unknowable artistry of Japan, the source of his profound, confusing love for the land.

On Thursday, April 22, 1858, a prestidigitator—a magician—was summoned to perform for the exhausted diplomats. A clown beat drums and a flute player piped, creating a strange, hypnotic rhythm. Then the man with the completely shaved head took the stage.

He performed tricks that seemed utterly divorced from the world of logic and reason that Henry and Harris fought to impose. With the sole aid of his fan, the man seemed to make small butterflies appear, flutter about in the air, and rest on flowers. He did this for over an hour, holding the two Americans' attention with a dazzling, impossible display of control and mystery.

For Henry, it was a moment of intimate entanglement with the country's soul. This was the Japan he adored—the land of flawless grace and impenetrable mystery, a civilization that could conjure life from air and make magic a reality. It was a secret world hidden behind the palace's official screens, a world that offered an escape from the deadly, black-and-white logic of the treaty.

The mission was now a race against the European Hammer and a struggle against the Japanese spirit itself, a spirit that could be as deadly as a rōh-nin's blade or as beautiful as a butterfly summoned by a fan. Henry Heusken was trapped between two impossible worlds: the logic of the West and the sublime, murderous mystery of the East.

22

The Dutch Challenger

The silent, fragile truce in Edo was shattered by a polite, professional intrusion. On April 23, 1858, Mr. Donker Curtius, the Commissioner from the Netherlands and the sole Western diplomat previously allowed a permanent residence in Japan, arrived in the capital. The race had begun.

Henry felt the immediate tension of the situation, complicated by a profound personal ambivalence. Curtius, accompanied by his secretary, Mr. de Graeff van Polsbroek, represented Henry's homeland—the country whose flag he had left behind to chase the American dream. He rode out immediately to pay a visit to the rival, the formal exchange of a layer of polite armor over the shared anxiety of being Western exiles in this enormous, hostile land.

Harris, physically recovered but mentally exhausted by the Mikado's political veto, understood the stakes better than anyone. The United States had fought for two years to win a *fair* treaty—one based on mutual benefit and the Law of Nations. If Curtius or a more aggressive power like England or France signed a weaker treaty first, that would set a precedent, and the principles Harris held dear would be lost. The American treaty had to be the framework.

The Ritual and the Ruse

The official visit to Shinano no Kami on Monday, April 26, confirmed the intensity of the moment. Shinano received them with a rigid Japanese dinner—fish, chicken soup, and quail arranged with their feathers—but Henry's focus was on the noble's household. He saw the archery range, the tiny, manicured garden, and the apertures in the windows through which the forbidden women of the household peered out, observing the foreign devils. They were allowed to be seen only by other women, young shorn boys, and men whose heads were completely shaved like scholars—a poignant reminder of the social cage that confined the Japanese female spirit.

Henry's time was split between the political game and a necessary escape. His late-night rides became a ritual of absorption. With ten lantern bearers illuminating his path, he traversed the capital, hearing the clanging of the police officers' iron staffs, the sounds bouncing off the castle walls, which stood reflected in the moat.

On Thursday, April 29, Henry and Harris visited the great Kannon Temple, a necessary act of cultural observation. It was a place of divine confusion and human commerce, a fair where shops lined the broad avenue. Henry was struck by the raw contradiction of the Japanese soul: the temple housed idols, curious objects, and paintings of the beauties of the Yoshiwara (the notorious pleasure district). In one booth, he saw figures made of tortoise shells, including a man who greatly resembled a Dutch burgomaster of the 17th century—a ghost of the old, closed-off Dejima trade era. Another booth displayed an enormous collection of nude female figures, openly exposed to the public gaze. The blend of sanctity and profanity was absolute.

The Illusion of Control

The pressure from the Daimyo continued to mount. The Mikado's refusal to sanction the treaty had emboldened the xenophobic elements, yet the Shogunate tried to maintain the illusion of control. Harris and Henry were treated to Javanese luncheons and, again, the sight of a prestidigitator.

The bald-headed sleight-of-hand magician, working only with his fan, made small butterflies appear, fluttering about the room. It was a dazzling, symbolic act that captured Henry's imagination: the essence of Japanese power, capable of creating exquisite illusions but currently unable to exert tangible political control over its own princes. The illusion was beautiful, but the reality was lethal.

On Tuesday, May 18, 1858, the political crisis peaked. Higo no Kami returned from Kyoto, confirming the worst: the Daimyo opposition was overwhelming. Placards were posted: "We shall kill Hotta, Bitchū no Kami." The Mikado was now fearful and would only follow the Daimyo's lead. Hotta was constantly negotiating in Kyoto, but the core issue remained: "if they should sign the treaty now, a rebellion would certainly follow."

The Final, Forced Move

The Shogunate, aware of the imminent arrival of the European fleet, found itself cornered. On May 15, 1858, Harris, seizing the moment, wrote a decisive letter to be held at the U.S. Consulate in Shimoda, intended for the first American warship to arrive. The letter requested that the ship proceed to Edo Bay. Harris was fully aware that the Japanese might read the letter—and he had no objection to it. When the Japanese agreed to deliver it, they did not object, quietly signaling their preference for the measured pressure of the Americans over the more aggressive postures of the English or French.

The political struggle continued through June, with Harris pushing, cajoling, and finally suggesting an ultimatum: sign to-morrow, dating the documents three months hence. This would allow the government to declare the treaty executed, while giving the Mikado and the Daimyo three months to accept the fait accompli.

On Tuesday, June 8, 1858, Henry met with Curtius, who revealed that the Japanese had offered him the same advantages and a copy of the American treaty. Curtius was maneuvering to sign a less-demanding treaty first, thereby setting a weaker precedent.

Harris knew the game was lost unless he forced the signature on the U.S. treaty. The arrival of an American warship would give him the necessary, non-negotiable leverage. The time for diplomacy was over. The time for the European Hammer—wielded by the only American in Edo—had arrived. The treaty would be signed at gunpoint, but it would be signed on American terms.

The situation has reached its absolute breaking point.

"The deepest truths are not written, but remembered."

June 8 marked Henry's final entry in his daily journal—a record he would not resume until January 1861, nearly three years later, when he picked up writing again in the very same volume. The following day, June 9, Harris too ceased his daily entries.

The near-simultaneous silence of both men is striking. For years, they had been meticulous diarists, faithfully recording their experiences, frustrations, and reflections in a land still largely closed to the West. Yet, suddenly and without explanation, both pens went still.

Why did they stop? Was it mere fatigue, the monotony of waiting for the treaty's full implementation, or something more deliberate? Perhaps they suspected that their journals were being read by Japanese officials, or feared that their written thoughts revealed too much about their opinions, emotions, and negotiations.

In a country where the written word carried binding weight, where even a single line on paper could fix one's position or betray one's heart, silence may have felt like the safest form of discretion.

We cannot know for certain what caused these two men—so diligent in their recordkeeping—to fall silent almost in unison. It remains one of the more curious mysteries of their time in Japan. Yet, while their daily journals—the lifeblood of this narrative—ended in June 1858, their story did not.

Through letters, dispatches, and other historical records, we can still trace the path of Henry's life and work as the months and years unfolded. What we lose, however, is the intimate voice of the man himself—the private reflections, doubts, and emotions that only a journal can reveal.

As an old saying reminds us: "The deepest truths are not written, but remembered."

23

The *Powhatan* and the Signature

The agonizing wait in Edo ended not with a letter, but with the inevitable: the arrival of a U.S. warship in Edo Bay. It was a sad necessity, a brutal reminder that diplomacy, for all its sublime rhetoric, sometimes required the cold language of cannon fire. The American warship USS *Powhatan* steamed into Edo Bay, her black hull and imposing firepower an explicit, silent endorsement of Harris's demands.

Townsend Harris, who had suffered fever and diplomatic fatigue for two years, understood the urgency of the gunboat's presence. The threat of the Cannon was no longer a negotiation tactic; it was reality. Curtius, the Dutch Commissioner, was close to securing a rival treaty that would grant him "the great credit of having made the first Commercial Treaty with Japan," thereby securing all American concessions for Holland while denying the United States its rightful place in history.

Harris, ever the master strategist, had already taken the ultimate precaution. He knew that breaking off negotiations would allow Curtius to step in immediately, crippling future American efforts.

Instead, Harris presented the Council of State with his final, non-negotiable ultimatum: pledge in writing not to sign any Treaty or Convention with any other authority until the expiration of thirty days after signing the American Treaty. The Japanese, cornered by the Mikado's refusal to sanction the treaty and the physical presence of the American warship, acceded to the proposition.

The Signature of Destiny

The final act of the two-year odyssey took place not on the paper-matted floor of the Shogun's palace, but on the hard, familiar deck of the American warship. On July 29, 1858, the Commissioners were brought aboard the USS *Powhatan* in Edo Bay.

The signing of the Treaty of Amity and Commerce—the Harris Treaty—was a scene of immense, almost unbearable contradiction. The Japanese officials, in their severe ceremonial dress, were surrounded by the steam and steel of American naval might. The moment was one of tremendous relief for Harris, yet it was tempered by the acute, bittersweet awareness that this triumph was achieved by the very force he had tried so hard to avoid.

Henry stood at the center of the world, his Dutch tongue the only bridge over the vast chasm between the kneeling Japanese officials and the triumphant American Commodore. Every clause, every word of the document that would redefine Japan's history, passed through his mind and voice. The silence in the cabin was broken only by the scratching of the pens—the Shogunate's final, bitter surrender to the inevitable.

Henry's Global Validation

The moment the ink dried on the treaty, the political dam broke. Japan was now open, and the other European powers descended to secure their own deals. Within thirty days of the American signature, the Japanese authorities finalized similar commercial treaties with the Netherlands, Russia, and Great Britain, but they did not achieve them on their own.

By this time, Henry had become the central figure in the European efforts to open Japan. While Harris had led the U.S. mission and struck the first formal steps toward engagement, it was Henry who now worked to extend those openings to other nations. He understood that the vision of free commerce was not meant for the United States alone; it was a principle to be shared, a foundation upon which all nations could build. If any single country gained a monopoly on influence, it might sow the seeds of future conflict.

Instead, Henry sought to ensure that what the United States had begun—the framework of trade, diplomatic relations, and even friendship—could be used fairly by all nations, establishing a stable and lasting network. Harris, for his part, was content to step back, allowing Henry to be the architect of this broader expansion. He recognized that Henry's careful work in extending free trade and mutual understanding was exactly what Harris himself had hoped to achieve, yet now executed with a steadiness and reach that Harris, for all his ambition, could not command alone.

Harris, in a remarkable act of professional generosity and strategic pragmatism, made Henry indispensable to the world. He offered Heusken's services to Lord Elgin, the British Ambassador. Henry, the once-penniless young man from Amsterdam, was now interpreting, advising, and guiding the diplomats of the world's most powerful empires through the complexities of the Japanese court.

Lord Elgin, recognizing the extraordinary talent before him, gave Henry the ultimate validation in a letter dated August 27:

"I have found Mr. Heusken not only well qualified as an interpreter, but in all other matters in which I have had to refer to him, both intelligent and obliging in the highest degree, and I shall not fail to convey to Her Majesty's Government my sense of the importance of the aid which you, Sir, and your Secretary have rendered to me at this conjuncture."

Henry was no longer just Harris's secretary; he was acknowledged by the British Empire as an intelligent, indispensable figure on the world stage. The U.S. Diplomat had been validated by the Old World he had left behind.

24

The Solitude of Shimoda

The period between signing and implementing the treaty marked a lull in activity for both Harris and Henry. During this interim, both men ceased writing in their daily journals, suggesting a stretch of monotony and stagnation as they remained confined to the U.S. Consulate in Shimoda. They were well aware that they could not proceed to Edo until the treaty officially took effect in July 1859, leaving them in a state of enforced idleness.

For Henry, this pause may have provided an opportunity to refine his study of the Japanese language. He had already begun learning it prior to this downtime, and it is likely that he used these months to practice and improve his skills with anyone willing to assist him. Harris's experience during this same period was markedly different. His health, already strained by years of arduous diplomatic service, began to deteriorate further. By March 1859, the long mission had taken a visible toll, and Harris suffered from chronic dyspepsia—a condition characterized by persistent upper abdominal discomfort lasting for months. Though not typically accompanied by nausea, vomiting, or diarrhea, it was nonetheless debilitating. The illness left him physically weakened and added a personal burden to what was already a taxing diplomatic assignment.

In late March 1859, the USS *Mississippi* anchored in Shimoda Bay. Harris, under the care of Naval Surgeon John S. Fox, decided on a radical prescription: combining official business in Nagasaki with a much-needed vacation on the China coast. Henry, his indispensable shadow, was conspicuously left behind to handle routine matters at the Shimoda consulate.

Harris departed for Nagasaki, where he inspected sites for American residences—anticipating the commercial boom Henry had helped unlock—and was officially informed of his elevation from Consul-General to the grander title of Minister Resident. He would return two months later, improved in health, ready to move the Legation to the open port of Kanagawa.

For Henry, this departure was not a promotion; it was solitude. He was alone, utterly and finally, in the compound that had been both his prison and his professional forge for three years. The immense intellectual pressure of translating diplomacy was gone, replaced by a vacuum of domestic idleness.

The Forbidden Desire

The empty rooms of the consulate echoed with a silence Henry had never experienced. He was twenty-seven, robust and charming, and for years, his entire existence had been centered on duty, mission, and the unwavering moral authority of Harris.

Harris, the stern, principled mentor, had made his views on relationships with local women clear. Such liaisons, common among Western diplomats and merchants (Henry recalled the example of Edmund Blundell, the British administrator who had eleven children with his Burmese mistress), were viewed by Harris as morally corrupting and politically dangerous.

But with the treaty signed and Harris gone, Henry's disciplined mind could begin to rebel. He had not truly *seen* a woman in years, save for veiled glimpses behind blinds or the terrified faces that fled his approach on the Tōkaidō. Yet, in those rare moments, the beauty of the Japanese women—their delicacy, their composure, the quiet grace of their movement—had struck him with an overwhelming force.

He may have realized the immense irony: he had successfully opened the nation to the world, yet he was barred from its most intimate, human connection. His soul yearned not just for physical comfort, but for the profound entanglement with the culture he had come to love.

The Riddle of Courtship

Henry would have known a direct approach was impossible. Japanese society was a fortress built on protocol and etiquette, especially for the samurai and wealthy merchant classes, whose women he admired. He could not simply approach a woman; such an act would be seen as barbaric, a gross offense to her family's honor, and a confirmation of every Japanese fear about foreign vulgarity.

If he were to find a connection, it had to follow the rigid process—the deliberate, refined dance of courtship. He needed an intermediary—a *nakodo*—and he needed patience.

Henry could have begun his subtle, secret quest by approaching Japanese friends he trusted in the small town near the consulate. Most likely to his frustration, none were willing to serve as a matchmaker, fearing the consequences of facilitating a for-bidden liaison with the *gaijin*.

Yet, they may have been courteous enough to explain the intricate rules that governed romance in Japan. Above all stood the primacy of family—romantic love was secondary to duty, and no pursuit of affection could occur without the family's consent. To court a woman without her relatives' approval was unthinkable.

Then came the art of subtlety, a discipline that required emotion to be hidden behind gestures of restraint. Passion was not declared openly but hinted at through small, thoughtful gifts—perhaps a seasonal sweet or an object imbued with quiet symbolism. The language of the soul found its purest form in poetry: the brief, delicate lines of waka or haiku became the proper channel for expressing feeling.

For Henry, an educated European linguist, this revelation must have been humbling. If he wished to express his heart, he would need to master the art of the three-line poem, for any-thing more direct might breach propriety—or even law.

Finally, there was the matter of worth. A man had to prove his refinement and cultivation before being deemed suitable. His knowledge of calligraphy, his grace in poetry, or his com-mand of the tea ceremony spoke louder than any declaration of love. Only through such demonstrations could one hope to win favor within the rigid, elegant confines of Japanese courtship.

Henry, standing alone in the quiet emptiness of the consu-late, must have felt the weight of a new and unexpected chal-lenge. He had mastered the complexities of diplomacy and the intricacies of the treaty, yet now he faced something far more elusive—the art of love in the Land of the Rising Sun. True to his unshakable resolve, he would not have turned away from the pursuit. His restless spirit, so long confined to the solitude of Shimoda, yearned for connection, for something beyond duty and negotiation.

That yearning—intense, human, and perilous—may well have sown the first seeds of division between Henry and his mentor, Harris. Their eventual rift would not be born of politics or protocol, but of something more profound: the unbridgeable differences of two hearts seeking meaning in a foreign land.

25

The Breach

When Harris finally returned from his vacation on the China coast, it was time for them to move to Edo. The arrival of the first American Legation in Edo in June 1859—now head-quartered at the Zenpuku-ji Temple in the Azabu district—should have marked the triumphant consolidation of their four-year mission. The treaty was signed, the flag was flying, and the diplomatic victory was absolute. Yet, it was precisely at this moment of triumph that the fragile, intense bond between Townsend Harris and Henry Heusken finally snapped.

The rupture occurred on a quiet day in July 1859, without warning, without public confrontation. Henry, the man who had risked his life, nursed his mentor through fever, and stood as the linguistic anchor for the world's most significant diplomatic coup, suddenly left the Legation.

Harris' response was one of profound grief and bitter suspicion. He wrote immediately to the Department of State:

"I regret to inform you that Mr. Heusken, my Dutch interpreter, left me this afternoon without giving me a single day to provide a substitute... I feel greatly grieved at this sudden parting with a person to whom I had become much attached and who had been my sole companion during my weary solitude in this country."

Harris, the stern Puritan who had endured so much physical solitude, was emotionally devastated by the loss of his "sole companion." He couldn't reconcile Henry's action with the man he knew, seeing the move as an act contrary to "the rules of propriety and integrity."

Harris's mind immediately leaped to intrigue, suspecting that "means were used to induce Mr. Heusken to act"—an outside force calculated to "embarrass and injure the interests of the United States." He could not yet conceive that the injury was purely personal, rooted in the human need for recognition.

The True Cost of Service

Henry's motivation could have been complex, a culmination of months of simmering resentment that had begun during his solitude at Shimoda.

Henry had observed Harris's near-fatal illness, his confession, and his own indispensable role as caregiver and acting plenipotentiary. He had been the U.S. Diplomat who secured the treaty, yet Harris's constant, overbearing focus on the mission had led him to take Henry for granted, failing to provide the public substantive recognition Henry believed he had earned.

Henry needed his mentor to recognize what he had done, not just with gratitude, but with the value in the form of compensation—the full, official acknowledgment of his worth. Having nursed Harris back from the edge of death, Henry understood that the father-son relationship had run its course. He had to strike out on his own, not just for independence, but for validation.

The Quick Return

Harris, desperate for his linguistic bridge, was forced to rely on the kindness of others, accepting the services of Mr. Cowan, the interpreter for the British Consul-General, Rutherford Alcock.

The interlude, however, was brief. Henry, having made his point and tasted the first necessary measure of independence, soon returned to his former employment. His resignation was not a permanent break, but a desperate, necessary plea for recognition that ultimately forced Harris to acknowledge his maturity and irreplaceable skill. The personal price of the diplomatic triumph had been paid, and Henry was ready to step back into his destiny, now as an acknowledged partner, not merely an aide.

The breach has been mended, but the emotional scars remain. Henry returns to Edo just as the ports are opening, coinciding with the immense rise in anti-foreign sentiment.

26

The Calculated Return

Henry Heusken's precipitate departure on July 4, 1859, also could have also been a calculated move—a final, successful piece of high-stakes diplomacy executed purely for his own benefit. The actual cost of the Breach was Harris's emotional devastation; the true purpose was Henry's financial security.

Henry had spent over three years in Japan, acting not just as an interpreter, but as a cultural instructor, a tactical advisor, and a caregiver. Yet, his compensation remained stagnant, a painful insult when compared to the superior status and compensation of other Western interpreters who lacked his acumen and experience. The contrast galled him. He was by now an "old Japanese hand," an indispensable master of the unique *patois* of Dutch used by the Japanese, whose knowledge was essential to the new legation.

Henry needed more funds, not for greed, but because if he was going to be a man capable of securing a bride and establishing a life in this rigid, class-conscious society, he needed to be a man with means. His move was a calculated ultimatum: increase his salary, or lose the indispensable key to the entire mission.

The Diplomatic Cover

Harris, isolated and professionally crippled by the sudden loss of his "sole companion," understood the severity of his position. He could not admit to the Department of State that his star interpreter had quit over pay; such a confession would make him seem incompetent and expose the Legation's vulnerability.

Instead, Harris provided diplomatic cover, framing Henry's return in a manner that had a curious ring of half-truth. He stated, in effect, that the entire episode was merely a misunderstanding: Henry had left under the impression that he had Harris's consent to do so and returned to service the moment he appreciated that his impressions were wrong.

This careful phrasing saved face for both men—Henry's rebellion was excused as a simple error, and Harris's command was seemingly restored.

The Claim for Compensation

The real battle between them was not waged in words or gestures, but on paper. Harris swiftly composed a long and forceful appeal to Washington, arguing for a substantial salary increase for Henry—an explicit acknowledgment that money lay at the heart of the growing tension. In his letter, Harris detailed the true extent of Henry's worth, which far exceeded his official title of Consul Interpreter.

He began by noting that Henry had lost five months of pay at the outset of the mission, as his salary only began in March 1856 despite his engagement the previous October. Since January 1857, Henry had borne the weight of all major negotiations, performing duties far beyond the narrow bounds of his position. His efforts had been critical to every diplomatic exchange, translating not only words but entire systems of meaning between two worlds.

Harris further stressed that Henry's most taxing responsibility had been serving as instructor to the Japanese interpreters themselves—men entirely unfamiliar with the intricate diplomatic vocabulary required for the Treaty of Edo. This task, demanding both patience and precision, had fallen solely upon Henry.

What truly set him apart, Harris argued, was his rare linguistic gift: a complete command of the peculiar form of Dutch used by the Japanese, a hybrid dialect shaped over two centuries of constrained contact with the West. Such expertise was irreplaceable.

Harris concluded, with the blunt practicality of a former New York merchant, that it would be impossible to retain Henry's services—or find a suitable replacement—for less than $2,500 a year. Moreover, he insisted that this merit not only an increase in salary going forward but also retroactive compensation of at least $1,500 for his past underpaid labor.

The Triumph of Means

Henry's gamble had paid off brilliantly. On January 1, 1860, his salary was raised to $2,500 per annum—a significant triumph that acknowledged his extraordinary value and gave him the financial means to establish himself fully.

Now a man of standing, both in wealth and reputation, Henry had become a celebrated diplomatic figure and the most accomplished interpreter in all of Japan. He returned to his post at the Edo Legation in the Zenpuku-ji Temple, prepared to enter the next chapter of his life—a chapter in which he could finally seek personal fulfillment amidst the rapidly opening world he had helped shape.

The emotional distance between him and Harris persisted, shaped by age, temperament, and the burdens of their long, exacting work. Yet the financial and professional terms of their partnership were now firmly secured. With his position stabilized, Henry was ready to step out from his mentor's shadow, equipped with both the resources and confidence to carve out a life—and perhaps even a love—in the land he had played a crucial role in transforming.

27

The Price of Otsuru

The return to Edo marked a turning point for Henry Heusken, particularly with the establishment of the American Legation at Zenpuku-ji Temple. The new post finally delivered the security and professional standing he had so fiercely coveted. He had achieved the status of a diplomat of consequence, finally escaping the shadow of the poverty that had once defined his youth. Yet, beneath the façade of success, his personal life remained desolate.

Heusken was a young man in his twenties, his soul still an "empty, echoing chamber," deeply scarred by the immense and prolonged solitude demanded by the isolated diplomatic mission. It was during this period of significant professional gain but persistent personal emptiness that Henry's life likely began to change more profoundly, for it was around this time that he is believed to have met Otsuru, the Japanese woman who would become his future wife.

The true identity of Otsuru remained shrouded in the soft, blurring glow of lantern light and the haze of Henry's deep-seated desire. It is highly improbable that she hailed from a high-ranking Japanese noble family. Instead, the historical context suggests she was likely a Geisha, a skilled mistress of delicate arts, or perhaps a high-ranking Courtesan, her beauty serving as her primary currency.

In the deepest recesses of his hungry heart, however, Henry likely did not care about her exact social standing. After four years spent in unrelenting isolation, devoid of the affection, touch, or laughter of a woman, her mere presence was enough to awaken a long-dormant hunger. It was a yearning that went beyond simple physical comfort; it was a desperate, immediate need for connection.

The Ritual of the Hanamachi

The immense pressure of the Treaty, the endless battle against Daimyo and Mikado, found its only release in the intimacy of the *hanamachi*—the world that operated entirely outside the strict, official clock of the Shogun.

In the 1850s, Edo had a well-established network of hanamachi, or "flower districts," which were officially sanctioned entertainment quarters where geisha and courtesans lived and worked. These districts were not merely centers of pleasure—they were cultural hubs that showcased traditional arts, music, dance, and elaborate etiquette, forming a distinct world within the city.

The most famous hanamachi in Edo was Yoshiwara, located in the northeastern part of the city. Yoshiwara had been relocated there in the early 17th century after the original district near Nihonbashi burned down. By the 1850s, it was a bustling, highly organized quarter, known for its licensed brothels (oiran houses) and teahouses (ochaya), where high-ranking courtesans and geisha entertained clients. The area was characterized by broad, tree-lined streets, elegant architecture, and a rigid social hierarchy that governed the lives of its inhabitants.

Life in Yoshiwara followed strict rules: courtesans and geisha underwent years of training in the arts of conversation, music, calligraphy, and dance. Patrons were entertained with sophistication and subtlety; the goal was cultural refinement rather than mere sensual pleasure. Seasonal events, festivals, and the display of exquisite kimonos and hairstyles added to the district's allure, making it a center of fashion and aesthetic taste.

For foreigners like Henry in the 1850s, hanamachi would have represented a completely foreign and highly controlled cultural world. Access to the district was limited, and interactions were often mediated by intermediaries. Observing the hanamachi offered insight into Edo's social structure, the role of women in entertainment, and the refinement and ritualized nature of Japanese pleasure culture—a sharp contrast to European notions of brothels or nightlife.

Henry might have met Otsuru in Yoshiwara while there with other young diplomats. What began as a formal visit, perhaps with friends, quickly became Henry's quiet ritual. Night after night, he began returning alone. The soft sound of her *shamisen*, the deliberate grace of her service, her laughter echoing within the small, polished parlor—all of it slowly stitched itself into the fabric of his desperate heart.

In Otsuru, Henry might have seen the very spirit of the nation he had fallen in love with: an exquisite, contradictory beauty, refined by tradition yet bound by contract. She was the one human being in Japan who looked at him not as the *gaijin* Ambassador's secretary, but as a solitary man seeking refuge.

The Diplomatic Sanctuary

The precise circumstances of Henry Heusken and Otsuru's first meeting remain unknown, obscured by the rigid societal divisions of the time. Yet the interaction itself was inevitable; years earlier, letters like Rice's had already highlighted the need for companionship among Western men, confirming that exchanges between the sexes were underway. Regardless of how it began, Henry was no ordinary patron. As a respected Diplomat, he was under constant scrutiny, and his actions carried a far greater political weight.

If he were to make Otsuru his wife, he must have fiercely refused to accept that their relationship would be merely fleeting and commercially defined. Perhaps a radical thought took root: he would defy Japanese convention, offer her a life better than any Japanese man could provide, and make her his own. The very idea of marriage was revolutionary, a concept that threatened to destabilize Edo's social order.

The means to pursue this impossible goal lay in Henry's considerable salary and his new diplomatic status. His plan was to bring Otsuru into his household, perhaps under the guise of a servant or companion—a necessary arrangement for a lonely American man. Henry understood the immense danger of exposure. Yet, Japan was a secretive society, a world of high walls. He intended to use his substantial pay and, crucially, his extraterritoriality—the legal shield he had fought so hard to secure—to lock himself away with Otsuru. This diplomatic immunity would place her beyond the Shogun's jurisdiction and safe from the judgmental eyes of the xenophobic populace.

The immediate and most challenging obstacle was Otsuru's contract. If she were a Geisha or a Courtesan, she belonged to a proprietor—a lord or madam who held the financial strings of her life. To secure her freedom, Henry had to initiate a new, deeply dangerous form of negotiation. This was a metaphorical treaty to buy a human soul, requiring more finesse and audacity than securing an international port.

Henry, the man who had mastered the value of the silver dollar and the language of international law, prepared for this ultimate diplomatic challenge. He would determine the price, make the offer, and secure the release of the woman who held the key to his happiness. The life-or-death mission of diplomacy had now culminated in the life-or-death urgency of the heart, risking political scandal for the sake of personal love.

It is almost certain that Harris would have disapproved of Henry's efforts. We can imagine Henry tried to keep the affair a secret, but Harris, sharp and observant, must have eventually discovered the truth. Yet, Harris likely remained silent. Confronting Henry would not only sever their working relationship but also destroy their personal bond, potentially causing Henry to leave his service once more. Harris knew that saying or doing anything to stop Henry would risk losing his invaluable companion and interpreter, and so he chose to look the other way.

28

Domestic Bliss and the Gathering Storm

The period immediately following Henry Heusken's reconciliation with Townsend Harris marked the zenith of his young life in Japan. His professional worth was now recognized, his position as First Secretary of the Legation in Edo was secured, and his personal life was anchored by Otsuru.

The two lived together in a profound state of Domestic Bliss. While the intricate circumstances of Otsuru's liberation and their union remained shrouded in the intimacy of a private home—perhaps a secret ceremony known only to them—the outcome was indisputable: subsequent accounts consistently referred to Otsuru as his wife. This domestic partnership provided Henry with the crucial stability and companionship that contrasted sharply with the profound isolation he had endured in Shimoda.

The Indispensable Companion

Henry was no longer merely surviving in Japan; he was thriving in the new diplomatic and business communities of Edo, Kanagawa, and Yokohama. In stark contrast to the socially isolated years before the treaty, he was now at the heart of foreign interaction, enjoying a rich social and professional life.

His fluency in Japanese improved, and his deep cultural acumen made him an invaluable resource to every arriving foreign power. Henry quickly became the preferred guide and companion for Western visitors, many of whom published accounts that universally noted the warm affection and high esteem they developed for him. His competence was so singular that he was frequently "loaned out" to other diplomatic missions, actively assisting the Prussian mission in their negotiations for a treaty with the Japanese government. Henry Heusken was, at last, fulfilling his true potential as a U.S. Diplomat—the living, breathing bridge between the West and Dai Nippon, "great Japan."

The Stolen Privilege

Henry adopted the customs and privileges of the nation he had embraced. He maintained an active lifestyle in the capital, continuing to ride horseback on his daily trips around Edo. This was not merely leisure; it carried a particular cultural weight, as horseback riding had historically been the exclusive privilege of the samurai, the warrior class.

To the influential, xenophobic samurai and lords—men fiercely devoted to seclusion (*sakoku*)—Henry, a young Westerner, engaging in their traditional activity in the capital was a visible sign of the profound changes sweeping the nation.

Henry's public display of this privilege was an insult, a symbolic usurpation of their authority by the invading *gaijin*.

The Shadow of Anti-Foreign Sentiment

But Henry's personal success existed under the lingering shadow of escalating danger. The recently signed commercial treaties, the very instruments of his triumph, had deeply angered Japanese subjects devoted to traditional policy.

This anti-foreigner sentiment was compounded by a second, equally lethal faction: those fiercely opposed to the ruling Tokugawa Shogunate. They recognized that the Shogun's weakness in the face of Western demands was a vulnerability they could exploit. By using the treaties as proof of the Shogun's failure to protect Japan, these rebels sought a pretext to overthrow the Tokugawa regime and restore the Emperor to political power.

Foreigners, particularly Henry, became targets in a much larger, internal political conflict. His fulfillment, his professional status, and his very presence were a threat to the nation's survival. Henry Heusken was having a marvelous time—but that vibrant personal existence was in deadly, chilling contrast with the political storm brewing around him.

29

The Shadow of the Rōh-nin

The years immediately following the opening of the treaty ports in 1859 were marked by a terrifying escalation of violence. Henry Heusken's newfound happiness with Otsuru existed in a fragile bubble, constantly threatened by the rising tide of the Sonnō Jōi—"Revere the Emperor, Expel the Barbarians"—movement. The diplomatic success that had won Henry his fortune and his wife was now the cause of a deadly, calculated campaign of terror.

The assassins were typically rōh-nin—masterless samurai zealots from powerful, anti-foreign domains like Mito and Satsuma—and their targets were the foreign presence itself, executed often in the night near the Legations in Edo and Yokohama. The six foreigners assassinated in the eighteen months before January 1861 were victims of this rising tide of anti-foreign and anti-Shogunate fury.

The Pattern of Blood

The atmosphere in Edo was turning lethal, driven by a clear political calculus. Every murder was a calculated statement designed to provoke a crisis, discredit the weak Tokugawa Shogunate, and ultimately force the expulsion of all foreigners. Henry Heusken watched in horror as the pattern of targeted violence began to close in, suggesting that no European life was truly safe.

The initial danger emerged swiftly with the opening of Yokohama. In quick succession, Russian Sailors were murdered in the port vicinity, an act soon followed by the killing of a Dutch Merchant Captain. This violence chillingly proved that the threat was neither confined to a single nationality nor limited to the guarded confines of diplomatic compounds. The assassins sought to terrorize the entire foreign community.

The threat became intensely personal with the assassination of Kobayashi Denkichi on January 29, 1860. Kobayashi was a Japanese interpreter working for the British Legation, a figure who had lived abroad, mastered English, and served as a vital cultural intermediary between East and West. Two samurai just outside the British Legation at Tōzenji Temple in Edo fatally wounded him.

For Henry, himself the most crucial interpreter in Japan—and currently assisting Count Friedrich zu Eulenburg's Prussian Mission—Kobayashi's death was a grim, terrifying mirror of his own potential fate. Kobayashi's crime, in the eyes of the radical samurai, was the facilitation of the foreign presence; Henry's crime, as Harris's chief aide, was being an architect of that presence. The message was unmistakable: those who bridged the cultural gap were marked men.

The Shogunate's Collapse

The assassination plot ran parallel to the collapse of the Toku-gawa regime. The most significant symbol of this internal polit-ical breakdown was the murder of the Shogun's chief minister, Tairō Ii Naosuke, who was assassinated less than ten months before. Ii Naosuke was the official who had ultimately forced the treaties through. His death underscored the deadly reality: no official was safe.

The Shogunate faced an impossible dilemma. Foreign powers demanded that the treaties be upheld, threatening military force if their citizens were harmed. Conversely, powerful, xenophobic Daimyō viewed the treaties as a national disgrace that brought pollution to the sacred soil of Japan. The Shogunate's officials, whom Harris dealt with daily, were caught between Western gunboats and domestic assassins.

The Mentor's Fear and Henry's Defiance

Townsend Harris, the man who had once furiously demanded the removal of the Japanese "spies" who guarded the Legation, now possessed a deep, desperate appreciation for their role. He understood that harsh Western demands only fueled the Daimyō's anti-foreign outrage.

Harris, most likely, pleaded with his First Secretary to be cautious, urging him not to venture out at night and to be armed to the teeth with guards when traveling. The diplomatic rules were reversed: the guards were no longer spies but poten-tial saviors.

But Henry, buoyed by his youth, his happiness with Otsuru, and his successful defiance of custom, was perhaps too confident in his immunity. He was a man of the light, accustomed to riding his privileged horse through the capital, demanding his right of way. He was the vital figure for the Prussian mission, the indispensable guide for foreign nobles.

The extremists, who aimed to demonstrate that treaty-making was a deadly path, needed a victim of high profile and obvious symbolic offense. Henry Heusken, the American who had achieved too much, was the perfect target.

/ 30

The Last New Year's Ride

The calendar had turned to January 1, 1861, marking the final New Year of Henry Heusken's astonishing, brief life. He was, undeniably, riding the crest of his personal and professional fulfillment. Heusken was now a man of means, his handsome salary a concrete representation of his value to the diplomatic community. Professionally, he was the most effective diplomat in Japan.

More profoundly, Henry was no longer lonely; he was a father. Though the name of the child remains unrecorded in the world's official journals, Henry knew that back at the Legation, his beloved Otsuru cared for their son—a final, complete realization of the family life he had once only dreamed of achieving.

It was on that New Year's Day that Henry, for reasons unknown, picked up his personal journal again, placing in it the first entry since June of 1858. That marked an interval of approximately 2.5 years (30 months) without writing. Why he chose this moment to suddenly resume journaling remains a profound mystery, yet it is a decision timed with tragic irony. One can only wish he had taken up his pen earlier to chronicle his courtship with Otsuru or to celebrate the birth of his child. Instead, his first journal entry in years served as a dark foreshadowing, reflecting not his personal joy, but the growing crisis and volatility gripping Japan.

The Mito Plot

On January 1, 1961, Henry writes that he was going to see Townsend Harris, who was staying at the home of Consul Dorr in Kanagawa, which should have been a simple New Year's courtesy. Instead, it was violently interrupted by the cold shock of political reality. A Governor of Foreign Affairs arrived, sent expressly by the Great Council to deliver a message in absolute, terrified confidence.

The message was an apocalyptic prophecy delivered by the government itself. The Shogunate had learned of a clear and lethal plot: five or six hundred rōh-nin, followers of the fiercely xenophobic Prince of Mito, were organizing a coordinated attack.

The catalyst for this organized terror was the very export trade that Henry's treaty had mandated. Foreign demand was causing the price of food staples to rise constantly, inflaming the populace. The rōh-nin's objective was total chaos: to burn Yokohama to the ground and to attack the diplomatic Legations in Edo and the consulates in Kanagawa.

The government's response was a confession of its own political paralysis. They had ordered two Japanese steamers to stand by—a pitiful defense. Two friendly Daimyo had sent six hundred men to protect the merchants of Yokohama. But for the core diplomatic legations, the only security offered was an order: Ministers and their attachés should retire to a house situated within the compound of the Imperial Palace in Edo. The Shogun was asking the foreign diplomats about the cause of the crisis, inviting them to become his guests and prisoners in the safest fortress in the entire Empire, shielding them from the Shogun's own rebellious vassals.

Harris, the old hand, instantly perceived the severity of the crisis. He dismissed the Governor's panic, claiming he did not think the matter was so serious, but his actions betrayed his terror. He immediately dispatched Henry—the visible, indispensable messenger—straight into the eye of the brewing storm, to inform the other Foreign Missions of the plot. Henry's duty was no longer simply to translate, but to coordinate the entire Western response against the forces that sought his life.

The Final Work

On January 3, 1861, the Prussian Treaty, which Henry had labored on for months with Count Eulenburg, was definitively concluded. But the atmosphere was heavy with death. The rumor circulated—and was politically denied by the government—that Hori, Oribe no Kami, a high-ranking official, had committed *hara-kiri* on New Year's Eve. The political system was eating itself, and the price of the treaties was mounting in ritual suicide.

On January 7, 1861, Governor Oguri, Bungo no Kami, visited Harris, claiming the general outlook was somewhat improved. But he revealed the government's utter helplessness: they had discovered the six hundred conspirators, yet had arrested only a few because doing so would cause too much confusion. The conspirators' influential rank protected them from the weak hand of the Shogun.

The Fight for a Bow

Amidst this lethal danger, Henry and Harris remained fixed on the symbolic battle for dignity. Harris, however, still refuses to let the official government guards stay inside the legation. Instead, they are stationed just outside the entrance. The new guards, though, are showing a small degree of disrespect to Harris, and when he passes in and out of the Legation, they refuse to bow to him.

Governor Oguri, embarrassed, admitted he could not compel the arrogant followers of the Daimyo to obey this simple command. "It is difficult to compel the followers of the Daimyo to do it. In time, perhaps!" The Governor, though, was not saluted when passing the Daimyo officers, revealing the genuine contempt of the samurai class for the Shogun.

Henry, the man who had fought against the indignity of prostration in the Palace, now fought for the dignity of a simple bow. He refused to let the hostile samurai violate the diplomatic honor of the Legation. This final, petty battle was, for Henry, the most necessary: a fight to compel the respect he had earned through his sacrifice, his knowledge, and his high status.

He was the useful man, the father, the diplomatic bridge. He was happy and living, riding the privileged horse that marked him for death, surrounded by the signs of his successful life. The final, terrifying confrontation was no longer a question of *if*, but of when and where the forces he had helped unleash would finally collect their price. Heusken had done his duty, and the shadow of the rōh-nin was now heavy upon him.

Despite the pervasive political danger and the ominous nature of his sudden return to journaling, Henry Heusken's last journal entry on January 8, 1861, offered no hint of impending doom. It was, rather, a completely normal entry, a mundane record of the daily tasks of a U.S. diplomat in Edo. The content centered on routine treaty negotiations, specifically dealing with the rights of the Japanese government to seize and confiscate suspicious articles. It also mentioned a letter he had just translated for the Prussian minister. Tragically, Henry's final recorded words were preoccupied not with crisis or fear, but with the dry, necessary details of international law and his professional duties.

31

The Final Gallop

The assassins chose the night of January 15, 1861, exactly eighteen months after the treaties came into force. The victim was Henry C. J. Heusken, the man who had translated the nation's future into existence. It was a cold, sharp Tuesday evening, and the political atmosphere in Edo was poisonous, the capital trembling under the rumor of the five hundred rōh-nin plot.

Henry, nearing his 29th birthday, was fulfilling his duty: he was returning home from the Prussian Legation, having finalized the treaty for Count Eulenburg. He was the "most popular of all members of the foreign community," a master of Japanese custom who moved easily where his mentor could not.

The Ambush

The attack was a sudden, brutal, and calculated strike against the foreign presence in Edo, launched around nine o'clock at night. Henry Heusken was riding with the best, though ultimately futile, protection the Shogunate could afford: a small escort of three mounted officers and four footmen bearing lanterns.

As Harris grimly reported to the State Department, the diplomatic party was suddenly assailed on both sides. The assailants—a group of seven fierce rōh-nin—struck first at the very things providing light and movement. The horses of the officers were immediately cut down, and the lanterns were violently extinguished, plunging the entire scene into sudden, absolute darkness.

Caught in the ambush, Henry—the skilled horseman whose privileged riding had often been viewed as an insult by the warrior class—was instantly overwhelmed. He was grievously wounded on both sides of his body by the keen blades of the assassins.

Instinctively, Heusken forced his horse into a final, desperate gallop, charging toward the sanctuary of the Legation and his home. He rode approximately two hundred yards through the dark, perilous streets, the adrenaline of terror and purpose masking the lethal severity of his wounds. His voice, once the essential bridge between civilizations, delivered his final, heartbreaking words to the officers struggling to keep pace: "I was wounded and that I was dying."

Seconds later, Henry fell from his horse onto the cold streets of Edo. The assassins, their chilling political statement delivered, instantly fled, melting easily into the shadows of the vast city.

The Mourning of the Father

Henry was brought to the Legation about half-past nine, carried by the distraught officers to the Zenpuku-ji Temple that served at the U.S. Legation. Townsend Harris, shattered by the sight of his "able, efficient, and faithful Interpreter" bleeding on the matting, acted with agonizing speed. He procured surgical aid from the

Prussian and English Legations, marshaling every resource of skill and kindness the foreign community could provide.

But all was in vain. The wounds were mortal. The man who had survived poverty, the high seas, and diplomatic isolation died shortly after midnight, at half-past twelve o'clock on the morning of January 16, 1861.

The immediate, official response was one of terror and profound apology. Governor Oguri Bungo-no-kami immediately expressed his horror and attempted to console Harris for the "great loss," swearing that no effort would be spared in the pursuit, arrest, and punishment of the assassins.

The government's official grief served only to mask a far more intimate tragedy. The political fury that claimed the life of the young diplomat did more than rob Harris of his most vital companion; it robbed a wife of her husband and a child of his father. Within the secluded chambers of the Zenpuku-ji Temple, one can imagine Otsuru and Henry's infant son left in the wake of an immense, unrecorded pain. The vibrant, fulfilled life Henry had constructed over four remarkable years was violently extinguished, replaced by a profound silence where there had once been the clamor of ambition and the warmth of love.

Ultimately, Henry Heusken paid the highest price for the opening of Japan.

This was diplomatic blood for trade.

The forgotten price of opening Japan.

3 2

The Political Funeral

The death of Henry Heusken, the most visible and well-liked member of the entire foreign community, instantly plunged Edo into a political crisis of the highest order. The diplomatic corps was shattered, gripped by shock and fear, and the Tokugawa Shogunate itself was utterly terrified of the international backlash.

But the loss struck no one harder than Townsend Harris. Though he had no family of his own, he had long viewed Henry as his "son," the loyal, invaluable companion who had shared his years of grueling isolation. The violent, senseless end of his young protégé shattered him completely. Yet, the devastation swiftly gave way to a consuming, righteous, cold fury directed at the Japanese authorities who had failed to protect the American Legation.

The morning of January 16, 1861, was spent managing the aftermath. The highest officials immediately visited Harris—Simme Boozen no Cami, Muragaki Awadsi no Cami, and Oguri Bungo no Cami, who came with a message of condolence from the Minister of Foreign Affairs, pledging that no exertions of the

Government should be wanting to arrest and punish the perpetrators. Their public sorrow masked a profound political terror: the rōh-nin attack was a direct, successful assault on the Shogun's authority, proving that the government could not protect the foreigners it had pledged to shelter.

Harris, heartbroken but firm, demanded swift justice and planned a funeral that would be not merely a burial, but an unprecedented political demonstration.

The Stand-Off

Just before the formal funeral procession was set to leave on January 18, 1861, Harris faced his final, personal confrontation with the Shogunate.

Simme Boozen no Cami, visibly fearful, approached Harris with an urgent request. He desired that I would not attend the funeral, as he feared I might be attacked.

The message was clear: Harris, the architect of the treaties, was now the prime target, and the Shogunate could not guarantee his safety in the streets of Edo. To attend the funeral was to invite a second, lethal confrontation that would plunge Japan into war.

Harris's reply was the resolute summation of his entire life's work:

"I answered that I considered it a sacred duty to attend, and that I should do so regardless of any danger."

He turned the threat back on the Japanese: "I warned him that if anything happened to me under such circumstances, his government would be held responsible."

Harris informed his colleagues—Mr. Alcock (British Minister), Mr. de Bellecourt (French Minister), and Count d'Eulenberg

(Prussian Envoy)—of the threat. They immediately rallied, resolved to attend, making the funeral an explicit, collective act of defiance by the entire diplomatic corps. The crisis had created a unified front against the Shogun's enemies.

The Grand Cortege

The funeral procession for Henry Heusken, which moved from the American Legation to the cemetery, was arguably the most elaborate and politically charged spectacle Edo had ever witnessed in recent years. It was a fusion of Western military discipline and Japanese feudal power, essentially a moving treaty intended to showcase the Shogunate's authority and remorse.

Leading the procession were the highest-ranking Japanese officials—five Cami, headed by Simme Boozen no Cami—each attended by a large train of followers and guards. Their conspicuous presence was a final, desperate act of official protection and apology, acknowledging the gravity of the assassination.

The body of Henry Heusken, borne on a bier, was draped with the American flag as a pall and solemnly supported by eight Dutch Marines, since there were no U.S. Marines there to do the job. The entire diplomatic and military community of the West was fully mobilized to show unified respect and outrage. The Colors—the American, English, French, Dutch, and Prussian flags, all draped in mourning—were carried by Prussian sailors and protected by six additional Prussian Marines. A solemn pace was set by the band of the Prussian Frigate *Arcona*.

Townsend Harris and Mr. de Witt, the Dutch Consul General, walked side-by-side as the Chief Mourners for the Dutch-American diplomat, followed closely by the Ministers of Great Britain, France, and Prussia. The unusual display and the solemn music attracted a large crowd of Japanese onlookers, yet the assembly remained quiet and orderly.

Townsend Harris, consumed by grief yet rigorously focused on his diplomatic duty, ensured Henry Heusken received a tribute commensurate with his service and the outrage of his death. Harris noted that he made "use of all the means at my command to pay due honor to the remains of a most faithful officer of the United States." The elaborate funeral was his calculated final act of respect, demonstrating to the Japanese authorities that the life of an American diplomat would not be taken without consequence.

Profound Sorrow

The sheer senselessness of the act compounded Harris's profound sorrow. In his private reflection, he wrestled with the incomprehensible motive behind the murder. "I am at a loss to assign any special motive that could have influenced the assassins of Mr. Heusken," Harris wrote, describing the victim's universally appealing nature. Henry was known to be "kind and amiable in his temper; he never used any violence towards the Japanese." Moreover, by "speaking their language, he appeared to be a universal favorite." The victim was not a man of confrontation but of connection, making his murder a chilling statement that the assassins targeted not an enemy, but the very possibility of peaceful understanding.

In the agonizing aftermath of the assassination, Townsend Harris burdened himself with a heavy sense of responsibility for Henry's death. His grief was real and profound, yet mixed with self-recrimination over the warnings he had given but failed to enforce. "I have constantly warned Mr. Heusken of the danger he was incurring and prayed him not to expose himself in the manner he did," Harris wrote, the words dripping with regret.

He believed Henry's predictable routine made him an easy target. "For more than four months, he was in the habit of visiting the Prussian Legation, almost nightly," Harris noted, "and would return home from 8 to 11 o'clock at night." This "long continued and regular exposure," Harris feared, was precisely what led to the tragic end.

The emotional toll of the loss was immense. "I am suffering deeply from this sudden and awful catastrophe," Harris confessed, the absence of his young companion creating an unbearable void. Henry had been associated with him for over five years, and critically, was the companion of Harris's "long solitude at Shimoda."

In this moment of devastating loss, Harris finally articulated the true nature of their deeply intertwined lives, moving beyond professional titles to acknowledge their profound personal bond. "Our relations were rather those of father and son, than chef and employee," he wrote, a final, heartbreaking admission of the love and reliance he had placed on the young man whose life had been violently cut short.

The Private Grief

Amidst the grand, public spectacle of Henry Heusken's diplomatic funeral, the private grief of his family was utterly absent from the official record. There is no mention of his wife, Otsuru, or their young son attending the ceremony. They were, in all likelihood, confined within the Legation house, secluded and kept away from the world according to strict Japanese custom, unable to take part in the public honoring of their husband

and father. In this tragic way, Henry's brilliant public legacy—that of the essential, highly honored diplomat—had completely eclipsed his private love and family life.

Equally poignant is the complete absence of Otsuru and the child from Townsend Harris's official reports back to the Department of State. Harris, who had just lamented the loss of his "son," failed to acknowledge the immense, double loss felt by Henry's new family. While the reason for this omission is not explicitly stated, it is reasonable to assume that Harris did not endorse the interracial marriage and family.

His silence is likely rooted in his deeply conservative views on such relationships, which he had expressed elsewhere in his writings. This omission reveals the sad and ultimate failure of Harris's paternal bond: a father figure who could embrace the deceased son but could not accept the son's family. The official record, therefore, perpetuated the erasure of Henry Heusken's deepest, most personal commitment.

33

The Price of Blood

The solemn echoes of the Prussian band faded over the hills of Korin-ji, leaving Edo in a state of chilling calm terror at the close of Henry Heusken's funeral. The ceremony had not been a simple burial; it was a visible declaration that the war against foreigners had intensified, and the diplomatic world waited for the inevitable counter-stroke. Townsend Harris, back within the thin walls of the Legation, was consumed by a righteous, cold fury, refusing to yield to the panic that gripped his colleagues.

The foreign community, reeling from the murder of its most popular member, immediately favored an exodus. The general consensus was to abandon the dangerous streets of the capital and retreat to the coast, closer to the safety of the ships at Yokohama, fearing more victims of the rōh-nin's blades.

But Harris, despite the overwhelming grief that seemed to age him by ten years in a single week, flatly refused the counsel of retreat. He would not surrender Edo, the very city he and Henry had fought so hard and risked so much to enter.

He met the demands for withdrawal with unyielding logic. Harris contended that the Japanese authorities, though unable to guarantee absolute safety, were making serious efforts to uphold the treaties. To abandon Edo now, he argued, would be to validate the assassins and play directly into the hands of the anti-Tokugawa rebels. "The withdrawal of the legations from Edo to Yokohama might well eventuate in war," he declared. Harris, who had spent two arduous years preventing the very military solution that Commodore Perry had initiated, would not allow a rōh-nin's blade to destroy his carefully constructed framework of peace.

The Diplomatic Siege

The pressure on Townsend Harris to abandon Edo peaked when British Minister Rutherford Alcock arrived to demand an immediate withdrawal. Representing the formidable might of the British Empire, Alcock insisted that Henry Heusken's murder was definitive proof of the Shogun's impotence and demanded the complete retreat of the entire diplomatic corps. Yet, Harris stood absolutely alone against the consensus, refusing to discuss the matter further and declaring he would not, under any circumstance, leave.

The other foreign ministers—the French, the Dutch, and the Prussian—submitted to Alcock's dominant leadership. They withdrew from Edo to Yokohama, taking their national flags and their profound fears with them. Harris watched them go, remaining as the sole representative at the Shogun's perilous capital.

The retreating ministers soon learned the wisdom of Harris's stance. Within weeks, they realized that the Japanese populace and anti-foreign elements felt pleasure rather than regret at their absence. Their strategic retreat had achieved nothing but removing crucial pressure from the Shogunate to open and stabilize Japan. Forced to concede the diplomatic error, the ministers soon returned, acknowledging that Harris's single, solitary vigil had been the correct strategy. They understood that without his unwavering presence, they might have remained locked out of Edo indefinitely.

Harris's determination was rooted in more than just diplomatic strategy. Having witnessed the tragic death of his "son" on the Legation floor, he was consumed by a profound sense of grief and purpose that seemed to eclipse his own concern for safety. He was willing to make the ultimate sacrifice, just as Henry had for the mission, by refusing to yield ground. Ultimately, though, Harris did not have to make that final sacrifice. His unyielding resolve secured the presence of the foreign missions without costing him his life.

The Hunt and the Unsold Blood

Harris immediately put immense pressure upon the Ministers of Foreign Affairs, Kuze Yamato no Kami and Ando Tsushima no Kami, to bring the assassins to justice. The task was impossible. The difficulty facing the Shogunate was immense, and even Harris, the master strategist, knew the hunt was a political farce.

The assassins were rumored to be rōh-nin from the fiercely xenophobic domains of Mito or Satsuma. To pursue them meant directly confronting the most powerful elements of the Shogunate's opposition—a move that risked turning a cold diplomatic war into a hot civil war. The government was trapped between the gunboats of the West and the assassins of their own nobles.

The assassination of Henry Heusken carried a tragic irony that surpassed mere misfortune: of all foreigners in Japan, he was the one most sympathetic to the Japanese. He was the bridge, the fluent medium through which understanding flowed; yet, the forces of isolation chose him precisely because his presence was so successful, so convincing, and therefore so intolerable to their ancient order.

34

The Simple Headstone

The diplomatic corps, led by the British Minister, demanded a monument befitting a martyr—a headstone carved with the brutal details of the assassination, transforming the grave into a perpetual accusation against the Japanese nation.

Harris refused. His refusal was not an act of submission, but a final, protective gesture toward Henry's memory and the very essence of the mission. To inscribe the manner of death was to politicize the grave, to make Henry a perpetual weapon against the people he had grown to love. Harris chose a different path: a simple headstone bearing only his name and the dates of his birth and death. It was a profound statement of humility and respect, separating the man's sacrifice from the state's demands. Henry's final, physical manifestation in Japan would be an act of non-aggression.

The Currency of Grief

Henry's death had created a profound personal loss that required a material resolution, according to Harris. He knew that

Henry had been his mother's principal means of support for his entire adult life. He was determined to secure her future in Holland, where she had been her whole life, but he would not permit the payment to be seen as a cover-up for the murder.

In an interview with the Ministers of Foreign Affairs on November 25, 1861, Harris secured the final agreement: the Japanese authorities would pay $10,000 to Mrs. Heusken, Henry's mother.

Harris made his moral position clear: he put immense pressure on the two ministers, stating that they "must not consider this as a proposal from me to sell the blood of Mr. Heusken, or that the payment of any sum of money could be paid for his murder." The payment was compensation for lost income, not absolution for the crime. The authorities remained irrevocably responsible for delivering justice.

Over a year after the death, the letter arrived from Mrs. T. F. Heusken-Smit to Harris. Her words held the immense, simple weight of grief meeting Asiatic compensation:

"I have the satisfaction of informing you of the receipt of your many favors, the last of which... mented to me the happy success of your having obtained $10,000 from the Japanese government on my account, a great comfort in my sad circumstances, still deploring the loss of my tenderly beloved son."

The money, a vast sum in that era, was a great comfort—a pragmatic bandage applied to a profound, emotional wound. Yet, her deepest gratitude was reserved not for the coin, but for the act of love:

"But above all, I feel obliged to pay you my heartfelt thanks for your having erected a monument to my dear son's memory and your cordial homage often paid to him...."

The official transaction—the ten thousand dollars—secured Henry's European past, but it was the simple stone that spoke to the intimate core of their loss.

The Unwritten Future

Henry's mother was protected. But the final, aching irony remained the fate of Otsuru and the son. The $10,000 bought no security for them; their existence remained unrecorded, a silent casualty of the political storm.

The memory of Henry Heusken, the young man who knew too much and cared too deeply, was thus separated into two enduring legacies: one, enshrined in the American diplomatic record, secured by money and acknowledged by a plain stone; the other, an unrecorded, living silence—the Japanese wife and son, left to carry his name and his blood into the volatile, changing future of the Land of the Rising Sun.

35

The Ultimate Reckoning:
The New Japan and the Lost Heir

The blood payment had been made, the official grief discharged, and the simple stone laid to rest in the Azabu soil of Edo. Yet, the death of Henry Heusken was a debt that no ledger could truly settle, for it required the lives of the guilty. The Shogunate, weakened and desperate, could not simply apologize. It had to demonstrate, one final time, that it held the sovereign right to punish its own.

While the Tokugawa Shogunate's extensive police apparatus failed, at the time, to bring any perpetrator of Henry Heusken's assassination to justice, later historical investigation successfully uncovered the truth. The attackers were found to be members of a clandestine, radical group known as the Kobi no Kai—literally, the "Association of the Tiger Tail."

The Kobi no Kai was a fiercely nationalistic and anti-foreign political group active during the final years of Japan's Edo period in the mid-19th century. Composed primarily of low-ranking samurai and rōh-nin known as shishi (men of high purpose), the group adhered strictly to the Sonnō Jōi ("Revere the Emperor, Expel the Barbarian") ideology. Believing that the Tokugawa Shogunate had betrayed Japan by signing unequal treaties with the West, their primary goals were twofold: to restore political power to the Emperor and to expel all foreigners. To accomplish this, the Kobi no Kai engaged in political activism through violence, utilizing calculated, high-profile assassinations—such as the murder of Henry—to create chaos, discredit the shogunate, and ultimately provoke a reaction that would force the Westerners out.

Further research identified the specific individuals believed to have inflicted the fatal wounds on the diplomat, naming Masumitsu Shinpachirō (1841-1868) and Imuta Shōhei (1832-1868). Imuta, in particular, is reported to have delivered the massive abdominal wound that proved instantly fatal to Heusken.

In a grim twist of historical fate, none of the principal conspirators survived the turbulent era that immediately followed. Some, embracing the samurai codes of honor, later committed suicide, while others were themselves assassinated or died amidst the political chaos and bloodshed of the times. In short, even though the shogunate officially closed the case without arrests, subsequent research unveiled both the key network behind the attack and the names of the individuals responsible, whose ultimate fate reinforces just how turbulent and deadly the final years of the Edo period truly were.

The rōh-nin had won their ultimate, terrible victory.

The Retreat of the Patriarch

Townsend Harris, the Patriarch of Principle, stayed only long enough to witness the Shogunate's inevitable demise. He had submitted his resignation, his life's work finished, his spirit broken by the loss of the son he had found in his solitude. His final dispatches were filled with a grim prophecy: the Tokugawa regime was a ship taking on water, and no amount of treaty-making could save it.

Harris sailed from Yokohama aboard the USS *Niagara* in July 1861, heading back to the United States, leaving behind the diplomatic edifice he had constructed. He carried with him the heavy knowledge that his success—the forced opening of the gates—had hastened the very civil strife he had hoped to avert. He had saved Japan from foreign conquest, only to condemn the Shogunate to domestic collapse.

Though Townsend Harris left Japan without perfect health, he lived long enough back in New York to witness the seismic political shifts he had long predicted. Six years after the senseless murder of his protégé, Henry Heusken, the long-reigning Tokugawa Shogunate collapsed in 1867. The banners of the old, isolationist order fell, and the Meiji Restoration began—ushering in an era of profound, rapid change that finally embraced the modernity and international engagement Henry had championed. Harris's prophecy had been fulfilled: the Shogun's authority, undermined by the very treaties he was forced to sign, was utterly consumed by the forces of change.

The Meiji Restoration was a revolutionary moment that fundamentally transformed Japan's political and social structure. It marked the end of feudal rule by the samurai class and the restoration of direct imperial rule under Emperor Meiji. The new government, determined to establish Japan as a global power, immediately launched a sweeping modernization program. This involved rapidly adopting Western science, technology, political systems, and military organization under the rallying cry, "Enrich the country, strengthen the military" (Fukoku Kyōhei).

Crucially, the treaties that Henry Heusken had meticulously translated and negotiated—the very documents that the shishi had tried to violently annul—became the indispensable foundation upon which the New Japan was built.

Far from being destroyed, these agreements established the initial framework for diplomatic and commercial relations with the West. The new Meiji government, recognizing the futility of isolation and the necessity of Western engagement for modernization, did not tear up the so-called "unequal treaties."

Instead, they used the established ports and diplomatic procedures outlined in those documents to facilitate trade, opening channels for the influx of foreign technology, knowledge, and goods essential for industrialization. By accepting the terms, however humiliating, they also gained crucial time, focusing national energy on internal reform and strengthening the military.

Furthermore, the framework created by Harris and Heusken served as a blueprint for engaging with foreign powers, enabling Japan to quickly send diplomats and students abroad to absorb Western institutional knowledge and bring it back home. In this way, Henry Heusken's legacy was not erased by the assassin's blade; rather, the diplomatic structures he helped construct became a paradoxical yet essential stepping stone for the emergence of a modern, powerful Japan.

The Living Silence

Living on through diplomatic history is one thing, but living on through one's own blood is far more powerful—a truth reflected in the Japanese saying:

血は水よりも濃い

Chi wa mizu yori mo koi

"Blood is thicker than water."

Yet the fate of Henry's wife, Otsuru, and his only son remains an unanswered question. Their existence became a matter of unrecorded survival. With the protection of the Legation gone and the threat of rōh-nin vengeance against the family of the "traitor" still looming, Otsuru vanished into the vast, anonymous countryside. She carried with her only the memory of the fair-haired diplomat who had loved her and the precious burden of their child.

Perhaps Otsuru's final act was one of deliberate erasure. She raised her son under her own surname, suppressing his foreign heritage to ensure his safety and anonymity. The boy, part American adventurer and part Edo native, carried Henry's blood—the mingled heritage of Amsterdam and Azabu—into the volatile, transformative future of Japan, a secret heir in a country remaking itself.

In the end, nothing concrete is known of Otsuru and her son. All that remains is the hope that in the decades after Henry's assassination, the memory of Henry's kindness outweighed the political hatred that ended his life. Somewhere, someone must have safeguarded the legacy of his spirit, courage, and love—

the desire to see, to understand, and to connect—which lives on, binding Japan to the wider world. This unrecorded, unpunished lineage remains the final, enduring triumph of the man who knew too much and cared too deeply.

The Enduring Hinge

Today, the simple grave of Henry Heusken lies quietly, almost forgotten, in the cemetery of Korinji Temple in modern Tokyo. Untended and modest, it is a silent testament to a life of extraordinary intensity, abruptly cut short by the relentless currents of history. In just four and a half years, Heusken moved from an obscure interpreter to a pivotal figure in the opening of Japan, bridging cultures, languages, and worlds. His time in the country was brief, yet it was a hinge—a fleeting, vital moment between two long eras: the isolation of Tokugawa Japan and the transformative rush of the Meiji Restoration.

Though his body rests in a tranquil corner of Tokyo, the impact of his work resonates far beyond the temple walls. Through treaties translated, negotiations conducted, and relationships forged, Heusken became a conduit for dialogue between East and West, a living link between continents and cultures. The brevity of his life only sharpens the poignancy of his contributions. In those few years, he bore witness to—and helped shape—the awakening of a nation that had slept for centuries behind a veil of seclusion. His grave, simple though it is, marks the resting place of a man whose vision and courage quietly helped tilt the world toward a new age of connection, commerce, and understanding.